'Pon Top Edisto

Cookin' 'Tweenst The Rivers

Presented
by
Members and Friends
of
Trinity Episcopal Church
on
Edisto Island, South Carolina

As The Family Of God
Our Mission Is
To Proclaim By Word And Deed
The Good News Of Jesus Christ.

The recipes in this book,
though not always original,
have been tested,
altered, adapted, adopted, and enjoyed.
Many of these delicious recipes
have been handed down through
generations of Episcopal families.

Including recipes from
EDISTO ISLAND FAVORITE RECIPES
1972 – 1982 – 1990
by
The Women of Trinity Episcopal Church

Recipes kept from
EDISTO ISLAND FAVORITE RECIPES
are designated with a fish.

International Standard Book Number
0-9658723-0-0

Library of Congress Card Catalog Number
97-090451

Printed in the USA by

The Wimmer Companies
Memphis

'PON TOP EDISTO
INTRODUCTION

While most Edistonians are familiar with the history of our beautiful island, accounts of the preparation of her gifts from the sea and soil are few and far between. We know that explorer Robert Sandford was overwhelmed with the fields of maize when he first explored Edisto over three hundred years ago. It was not too long ago when new piles of oyster shells were "new finds" left behind by the Indians. And most of us know of the great feast prepared for the visit of Lafayette.

But even with the feast prepared for Lafayette, little is known other than the menu; and few, if any, recipes were ever written. The black people, who were shunned from learning to read and write, did most of the cooking and luckily the brilliance of their instincts was passed on to generations still living here. With our knowledge of history and those caring about the remembrances of the superior foods and cooks, *'Pon Top Edisto – Cookin' 'Tweenst the Rivers* is a welcome addition to all bookshelves.

Fewer places in the world can boast the agricultural superiority of Edisto Island and her semi-tropical location that has more species of plants than all of Europe. Surrounding these rich soils are the beautiful creeks, the feed of rivers, and the Atlantic Ocean. The ever popular term "lowcountry cuisine" could never have a greater home than Edisto, where the produce tastes better from the permeating salt air, the pristine waters have collections of abundant fish and shellfish, and a mystical aura encases it all. It is unthinkable for someone to visit and experience Edisto and to come away unchanged. And at the dinner table, one would be hard pressed to find another location with comparable offerings.

It is in this spirit that we embrace this collection of recipes from generations of Edistonians. It is an ambitious work that reflects the importance that not only Trinity, but all the churches, have linking their involvement with their flocks and food; for food is our restorative, our heart, and our soul. Wonderful families and volunteers have put their hearts and souls in this well-spanned gathering of popular Edisto recipes. It is my honor to have a written word in this introduction and to be included with all of the grand contributors.

Philip Bardin
Co-Proprietor/Chef,
The Old Post Ofice Restaurant
Edisto Island, SC

3

'PON TOP EDISTO
Cookin' 'Tweenst The Rivers
is dedicated to
THE GLORY OF GOD

Proceeds from the sale of the book
will be used for the
PRESERVATION & RESTORATION
of
TRINITY EPISCOPAL CHURCH
on
Edisto Island, South Carolina

SPECIAL THANKS TO:

RAVENEL GAILLARD
for his artwork from cover to cover

V. GUERARD
for the front cover, Trinity Episcopal Church,
and artwork throughout the book

ELIZABETH ALLSTON SMOAK
for her artwork, "The T'ree Seasons of Edisto"

AMELIA WHALEY
for the back cover, The Old King's Highway

PHILIP BARDIN
for the Introduction

N.C. "NICK" LINDSAY
for his enlightening explanation of 'PON TOP EDISTO

THE REVEREND BERT H. HATCH
for "The History of Edisto"

'PON TOP EDISTO
CONCERNING THE EXPRESSION

'PON TOP EDISTO is equivalent to standard American "On Edisto" and might answer the question, "Where do you live?" The P of *Pon* comes from the word *up*, so the whole expression rendered in standard American is "up on top of Edisto." In the same way, many expressions have found their way into standard American: The French noun *pois-pigeon* (= pigeon peas) becomes *hopping john* in standard American (= a cooked dish of field peas, rice, bacon, and onions). The French *de par Dieu*, = "de (les choses qui sont) par Dieu, (= this is from God, or, God did it) becomes *Debidue*, an island on the South Carolina coast. The Wolof verb *pat* (= to keep silent) has entered directly into standard American in the expression *stand pat*, not to budge from a position once you have taken it.

There's a valuable contrast between *in* and *'pon top* in certain similar sentences. (A) "I live in Nantucket Island / in the British Isles / in New York." The person is installed within the place, surrounded, protected, and with an implication of permanence. (B) "I stay 'pon top Edisto." The person is perched like a seagull on a piling, vulnerable to every wind and vigorous wave, and must notice the pattern of tides and sunsets just to stay there. Each moment includes something like a surf boarder's affirmation, "So far, so good."

The transience of real estate and the violence of God's mercy in hurricanes and other insurrections is not all bad in the language and concept that gives us " 'pon top Edisto." After certain recent buildings were constructed I heard on Edisto this expression which is well-known in Ghana, "Abomination has no remedy."

But, then, from Mrs. Ella Seabrook, the answer, "Never you mind. The Lord will prepare a *storm*."

What's just perched 'pon top Edisto will soon fly off.

Nick Lindsay

'PON TOP EDISTO
ANGELS

ARCHANGELS

Trinity Episcopal Church Women
Judie & John Nye
Captain John Kornegay
Maria & Steven Mungo
Barbara & Bill Hood

SPECIAL ANGELS

Catherine & George Arnot
Helen & Heyward Clarkson
Mary & Alex Crawford
Sally & Bob Currin
Carol & James Fowles
Nela & David Gibbons
Laura & Bill Hewitt
Pat & Darrell Jervey
Aimee & John Kornegay
Muff & Bill Lyons

Eliza & John Messersmith
Josita & Felix Montgomery
Dee & Larry Moss
Joyce & Harmon Person
Kathryn & Al Phillips
Van Leer & Buddy Rowe
Susalee & Bill Sasser
Nan & Bud Steadman
Suzanne & Parker Tuten
Ellen & Bubba Unger

GIFTED ANGELS

Wey Camp
Philip Bardin
David Foxworth
Joan Foxworth
Sammy Gaillard

Virginia Guerard
Bert Hatch
Nick Lindsay
Aimee Nelson
Beth Smoak

Amelia Whaley

'PON TOP EDISTO
COOKBOOK COMMITTEE

CHAIRMEN
Aimee Kornegay   Van Leer Rowe

SECRETARY – TREASURER
Judie Nye

FINANCE COMMITTEE
David Gibbons, Chairman
Wey Camp   Nela Gibbons

MARKETING COMMITTEE
Barbara Hood, Chairman
Bill Hood   Chip Hood   Frances Richardson

COMPUTER COMMITTEE
Aimee Nelson, Chairman
David Foxworth   Joan Foxworth

SCRIPTURE
Felix Montgomery   Josita Montgomery

ARTISTS
Samuel Ravenel Gaillard
V. Guerard   Elizabeth Allston Smoak
Amelia Whaley

WRITERS
Philip Bardin   Bert Hatch   Nick Lindsay

EDITING COMMITTEE
Catherine Arnot   Barbara Hood   Joyce Person
Gale Belser   Ellie Howard   Frances Richardson
Damaris Cardisco   Aimee Kornegay   Mildred Ann Rodwell
Weesie Fickling   Bo Lachicotte   Van Leer Rowe
David Foxworth   Aimee Moore   Ellen Unger
Joan Foxworth   Judie Nye   Martha Whetstone
Barbara Hamlen   Tag Wylie

'PON TOP EDISTO
BLESSING

As a preacher it is hard to extol the excellencies of heaven to those who know and love Edisto Island. Edisto is so beautiful and wonderful that God's glory comes shining through. This certainly applies to the food as well. As you will see, the heavenly banquet has always been previewed **'PON TOP EDISTO.**

I pray that our Lord Jesus Christ will bless the reader and user of **'PON TOP EDISTO** as He has blessed this Church and this island.

In closing, let me pass along this simple table blessing by the evangelist, preacher, scholar, and author, the Rev. Dr. John Stott at his birthday party.

Almighty God, our Heavenly Father,
in a world that is so hungry,
we thank you for good food,
in a world that is so lonely,
we thank you for good friends,
in a world that is so dark,
we thank you for the light of Christ.
Amen

God's Peace,
The Reverend E. Weyman Camp, IV

"It is like a grain
of mustard seed,
which a man took,
and cast into his garden;
and it grew,
and waxed a great tree."
Luke 13:19

'PON TOP EDISTO expresses its gratitude to the Episcopal Church Women of Trinity who planted the seed, nurtured it, and let it grow. The financial support of the ECW was most generous.

Thank each and every one who worked so hard, giving of their time, talents, and generous financial assistance.

Judith R. Nye
ECW President
1996 – 1997

'PON TOP EDISTO
TABLE OF CONTENTS

'PON TOP EDISTO
THE HISTORY OF TRINITY EPISCOPAL CHURCH

While the history of Edisto Island is told in terms of dates and events ... of wars and hurricanes and boll weevils ... the history of Trinity Episcopal Church, starting with the completion of the first church building on the present site in 1774 and continuing up to this very moment ... can only be told in terms of **people**. The happy brides and grooms married before Trinity's altar often became the owners and operators of Edisto's major plantations. The infants baptized at Trinity's font grew in both age and grace, sometimes to become leaders and shapers of Edisto Island life. And the funerals conducted in Trinity's sanctuary and graveyard were frequently indicators of the end of an important era in Edisto history.

The building built in 1774 was replaced in 1841, and that second building lasted for but 35 years, until it was destroyed by fire on February 28, 1876. The present building was consecrated by Bishop William Howe in 1881.

Throughout the years of its fascinating history, Trinity has seen its young men march off to war, some never to return to this blessed Island; it has seen its people beaten down in the face of hurricanes; it has known times of prosperity and times of want. This history has been recorded as it unfolded, in the laughter and the tears, the prayers and the ministries of its people.

From its inception until present day, Trinity Church has done *nothing* to change society or improve the quality of life on Edisto Island. What it *has* done ... consistently, beautifully, and well ... is to change its men and women, who have done and are doing the changing of society.

Bert Hatch

"Do not be anxious then, saying,
'What shall we eat?'
or
'What shall we drink?'
or
'With what shall we clothe ourselves?' ...
For your heavenly Father knows
that you need all of these things.
But seek first His kingdom
and His righteousness;
and all these things shall be added to you'."

Matthew 6:31-33

PLANTATIONS

'Pon Top Edisto

SUNNYSIDE
She-Crab Soup Sunnyside

BECKETT PLACE
Beckett Place Pecan Pie

BRICK HOUSE
Alice's Aspic

CASSINA POINT
French Toast a la Cassina

CYPRESS TREES
Shrimp Paste

FROGMORE
Macaroni Pie

MIDDLETON
Shrimp-Rice Pilau

OAK ISLAND
Oak Island Scalloped Oysters

PETER'S POINT
Peter's Point Tomato Catsup

POINT OF PINES
Overnight Crab Casserole

SEABROOK HOUSE
Seabrook House Oyster Stew

WINDSOR HOUSE
Mother's Ice Box Rolls

"He brought me to the banqueting house
and His banner over me was love."
Song of Solomon 2:4

SUNNYSIDE

SHE-CRAB SOUP SUNNYSIDE

¼ cup butter or margarine	½ teaspoon salt
2 tablespoons onion,	2 cups half-and-half
finely minced	3 tablespoons crab roe
1 pound crabmeat	⅛ teaspoon mace
2 heaping tablespoons flour	milk as needed to thin
Worcestershire sauce to taste	sherry to taste

- Sauté onion in butter over low heat until soft, but not browned. Add crabmeat and heat.

- Sprinkle flour, Worcestershire, and salt over crabmeat. Stir in half-and-half. Add roe and mace.

- Simmer slowly until thickened. Thin with milk to desired consistency.

- Add sherry to taste before serving.

Yield: 4 to 6 servings

Gale Belser

Sunnyside, constructed between 1875 and 1880 by Townsend Mikell, son of Isaac Jenkins Mikell of Peter's Point Plantation, is significant as one of the few remaining, relatively intact, immediate post-War Sea Island Cotton plantations on Edisto Island. Mikell adorned his house with a cupola, reminiscent of Bleak Hall, his birthplace and ancestral home of the Townsends.

13

BECKETT PLACE

BECKETT PLACE PECAN PIE

We make our pies from pecans we harvested and shelled from the trees we planted and cared for over the years.

3 eggs, beaten
1 cup sugar
½ cup dark corn syrup
1 teaspoon rum extract
   (or dark rum)

6 tablespoons butter or
   margarine, melted
1 cup pecans, pieces or halves
1 pre-baked 9-inch pie shell
   (350° for about 5 minutes)

- Combine eggs and next 4 ingredients and beat thoroughly; add pecans. Pour into pie shell.

- Bake at 350° for 45 minutes to 1 hour, or until done.

Yield: 6 to 8 servings

Bake several; they keep well in the freezer.

Ann and Tommy Nease

Beckett Plantation was established in 1709. The grounds were granted to the Lord Proprietors by King Charles II nearly 100 years before the Declaration of Independence was written. Today, all that remains are the tabby and handmade brick fireplace, headstones in the family graveyard, and an open well. There is also a large pecan tree, believed to be planted by the Becketts, which continues to bare pecans for our pies.

BRICK HOUSE
ALICE'S ASPIC

2 cups vegetable juice
2-3 bay leaves
1 teaspoon basil

1 teaspoon celery seed
2 tablespoons instant beef bouillon
2 packages gelatin

* Combine first 5 ingredients in a saucepan; heat slowly and simmer 10 minutes.

* Dissolve gelatin in water; combine with juice mixture. Pour into a greased ring mold. Chill until firm, about 2 hours.

Yield: 8 servings

Alice Hutson

Brick House was built around 1720 by Paul Hamilton. The bricks were imported from Boston and the lumber seasoned seven years. Said to be the first "Manor House" in America, Brick House was bought in 1798 by Joseph Jenkins and remains in the Jenkins family. Until it burned in 1929, it was the oldest house on Edisto Island.

CASSINA POINT
FRENCH TOAST A LA CASSINA

"French Toast a la Cassina has been a breakfast mainstay for our bed and breakfast. It was part of the first B&B breakfast that I cooked in 1990 and we continue to serve it today, seven years later."

6 eggs	dash of salt
2 tablespoons sugar	grated zest of 1 orange
1 cup orange juice	8 slices French bread
⅓ cup milk	(sliced ¾-inch thick)
1 teaspoon vanilla	butter to cook

- Combine eggs and next 6 ingredients and mix well. Dip bread slices in mixture; place in a single layer in a baking dish. Pour remaining egg mixture over bread; cover and place in refrigerator overnight.

- Bring to room temperature before cooking. Cook in butter in a skillet over medium heat until browned on both sides. Garnish as desired and serve with maple syrup.

Yield: 4 servings

Tecla Earnshaw

The plantation home at Cassina Point was built by Carolina Layfayette Seabrook and her husband, James Hopkinson, about 150 years ago. It remained in their family until the early 1980's. It is now cared for by Tecla and Bruce Earnshaw, who not only call Cassina Point home, but also offer Bed & Breakfast accommodations.

CYPRESS TREES
SHRIMP PASTE

2 (8-ounce) packages cream
cheese, softened
3 teaspoons onion juice
3 teaspoons celery juice
3 tablespoons lemon juice
2 teaspoons Worcestershire sauce
2 teaspoons horseradish

2 teaspoons mayonnaise
2 teaspoons heavy cream
2 dashes of Tabasco
1 teaspoon prepared mustard
3 teaspoons sherry
salt and pepper to taste
4 cups pickled shrimp, minced

* Whip cream cheese and add seasonings; mix well.

* Add shrimp and blend well.

Yield: 100 servings on crackers

Marian Murray

Cypress Trees Plantation became Clark property in 1728. Through the marriage of Susan Jane Clark and Dr. Joseph James Murray in 1858, the place became the Murrays'. The present plantation house was built in the 1830's. Additions and changes were made in 1906 and again in 1990.

FROGMORE
MACARONI PIE

2 eggs, beaten	salt and pepper to taste
1 cup canned cream	¾ cup uncooked macaroni,
1 cup water	cooked and drained
1½ teaspoons dry mustard	1½ cups grated sharp
1½ teaspoons Worcestershire	cheddar cheese
sauce	¼ cup margarine
½ teaspoon sugar	

- Combine eggs with next 6 ingredients. Add macaroni and stir in cheese. Place in a greased 8x8x2-inch casserole. Dot with butter.

- Bake at 350° for 30 minutes or until browned.

Yield: 4 to 6 servings

Adelaide Bailey

Long the home of Mr. and Mrs. Arthur Whaley Bailey, Frogmore is still held by the Bailey family. The property contains extensive plantings of blueberries, and in years past the public was allowed to pick the delicious blueberries.

MIDDLETON
SHRIMP-RICE PILAU

1 clove garlic, finely chopped	2-3 dashes of Tabasco
1 medium onion, chopped	salt to taste
1 bell pepper, chopped	1 cup shrimp, cooked and peeled
¼ cup margarine, melted	2 cups cooked rice
1 (8-ounce) can tomato sauce	

- Sauté garlic, onion, and pepper in margarine until tender. Add tomato sauce, Tabasco, salt, and shrimp; cover and simmer 10 minutes.

- Add mixture to rice; mix well. Place in a greased 2-quart baking dish.

- Bake, covered, at 350° for 15 minutes.

Yield: 4 servings

Caroline Boineau

Middleton was built by Dr. Robert Trail Chisolm for his wife, Mary Eddings, around 1815. During its early years it was known as The Launch and as The Chisolm House. It became Middleton Plantation when Dr. Chisolm's daughter, Susan, married Oliver Hering Middleton, third son of Goveror Henry Middleton in 1827. Its open and spreading design is characteristic of coastal plantations, where the climate influenced architecture, and covered verandas were necessities. Sand gnats are not a new invention. Middleton has been in the Pope family since 1902.

OAK ISLAND

OAK ISLAND SCALLOPED OYSTERS

1 cup round buttery crackers	1 teaspoon Worcestershire sauce
½ cup butter, melted	1 cup heavy cream
1 teaspoon salt	2 cups oysters, drained

- Combine cracker crumbs, butter, salt, and Worcestershire.

- Place half of mixture in a 1-quart baking dish or in 4 oven-proof seafood shells.

- Combine cream and oysters and spoon evenly over crumbs; top with remaining crumb mixture.

- Bake at 350° for 15 to 20 minutes.

Yield: 4 servings

Amy Connor

Oak Island Plantation house was built in 1828 by William Seabrook as a wedding gift for his son, William. Mr. and Mrs. Parker Connor are the fifth generation of the Seabrook family to own the Plantation. Before the War Between the States, the Plantation was known throughout the lowcountry for its magnificent gardens. Today the grounds are still celebrated for their great beauty through Mr. Connor's cultivation of over 400 varieties of camellias, which win countless awards each year.

PETER'S POINT
PETER'S POINT TOMATO CATSUP

This catsup is very good as a barbecue sauce on chicken, as a sauce with tacos, or any way you use catsup.

4 quarts Edisto tomatoes,   4 tablespoons salt
  peeled and quartered   3 tablespoons dry mustard
1 quart vinegar   1 tablespoon allspice
4 tablespoons black pepper   3-4 pods of red pepper

- Put tomatoes in a blender and chop.

- Mix tomatoes with vinegar and remaining ingredients in a large Dutch oven. Bring to a boil over medium heat and boil until thick, stirring frequently to avoid sticking.

- Bottle and cork while warm.

Yield: 2 quarts

This brings back memories of my mother, Caroline Simons Mikell, and my aunt, Eleanor Simons Lucas, on the back porch with a 10-gallon pot, a boat paddle to stir with, and a big bottle of vodka to make time pass.

Jenks Mikell

Isaac Jenkins Mikell built the house known as Peter's Point about 1840. Except for five years between 1861 and 1866, Peter's Point has been in the Mikell family's possession. In its day, the house was said to be one of the handsomest on the Island. She now dreams of her days of glory.

POINT OF PINES
OVERNIGHT CRAB CASSEROLE

1 pound crabmeat	1 can cream of mushroom
1 cup shell macaroni, small size,	soup, undiluted
uncooked	1 cup milk
4 ounces cheddar cheese, grated	1 tablespoon chives
2 hard-boiled eggs, chopped	2-4 tablespoons sherry

- Combine crabmeat and remaining ingredients. Place in a greased 1-quart casserole. Cover and refrigerate overnight.

- Bake, covered, at 350° for 1 hour.

Yield: 4 to 6 servings

Marian and Burnet Maybank

Point of Pines is where tabby ruins remain of the original fortification destroyed by the Spaniards in 1702.

SEABROOK HOUSE

SEABROOK HOUSE OYSTER STEW

3 tablespoons butter	salt and pepper to taste
½ cup finely chopped celery	10 saltine crackers, finely crushed
2 cups milk	1 pint oysters, drained
2 cups half-and-half	
1 tablespoon Worcestershire sauce	

- Melt butter in top of a double boiler. Add celery and cook for about 10 minutes. Add milk, half-and-half, Worcestershire, salt, and pepper. Mix in crushed saltines. Continue to cook until mixture is hot — do not let boil.

- Stir in oysters. When they begin to curl, they are ready. Remove from heat and serve immediately.

Yield: 4 servings

Four generations of the Dodge family at Seabrook Plantation have been blessed with wonderful cooking. First, Julia Brown presided over the kitchen, starting in 1929. Then Emily Meggett took her place and is still giving us much pleasure after more than 40 years. And, of course, we will always remember the remarkable Dorothy Harris.

Ruth Dodge

Seabrook House was built about 1810 on Steamboat Landing Creek by William Seabrook. Mr. and Mrs. D. D. Dodge completely restored the mansion, grounds and out buildings. The property is still owned by their descendants. History says that Seabrook House and The White House were designed by the architect Hoban, who practiced in Charleston in the 1790's.

WINDSOR HOUSE
MOTHER'S ICE BOX ROLLS

This is a great recipe for a holiday in that so much of the preparation is done before the "last minute".

1 package dry yeast	1 egg
1¼ cups warm water, divided	4 cups flour
1 teaspoon plus ⅓ cup sugar, divided	1 teaspoon salt
½ cup shortening	butter, melted

- Dissolve yeast in ¼ cup warm water and 1 teaspoon sugar; set aside.
- Cream remaining sugar, shortening, and egg. Add remaining water and beat. Add the yeast mixture and beat in flour and salt.
- Let dough rise in a warm place until it doubles. Punch down dough and refrigerate in a closed container until ready to roll out.
- Roll out dough on a floured board and cut into rolls. Place rolls in tins or in a pan and allow to rise.
- Bake at 400° to 425° for 10 minutes or until brown. Brush tops with melted butter and serve hot.

Yield: 18 rolls

After you punch dough and place in refrigerator, it will keep for several days.

Ellie Howard

Edward Whaley built this house for his son E. Mikell Whaley and gave it as a wedding gift. The construction of the house is cited between 1847 and 1857. It is a simple Sea Island style with high brick piers that provide an excellent view of Russell Creek and a welcome breeze. Union soldiers occupied the house during the War Between the States. Pictures, names, and graffiti have been found on the walls under old wallpaper in every room in the house. This plantation was the last to grow the long staple Sea Island cotton in the area.

EDISTO BREAKFAST SHRIMP

This is the classical lowcountry
"Shrimp and Grits" specialty!

½ pound shrimp, peeled
2 tablespoons fresh lemon juice
salt to taste
cayenne to taste
3 tablespoons bacon grease

¼ cup finely chopped onion
¼ cup finely chopped bell pepper
2 tablespoons flour
1 cup hot water, or shrimp or
    chicken broth

- Place shrimp in a bowl, sprinkle with lemon juice, salt, and cayenne; set aside.

- Heat bacon grease in a skillet; sauté onion and bell pepper over medium heat until onion is transparent, about 10 minutes.

- Sprinkle flour over vegetables, stirring constantly for about 2 minutes until flour begins to brown.

- Add shrimp and ¾ cup water or stock, stirring constantly and turning shrimp so they cook evenly. Cook for 2 to 3 minutes, until shrimp are cooked through and gravy is uniformly smooth, thinning with water, if necessary.

- Serve immediately with hominy.

Yield: 2 servings

Gale Belser

SAUSAGE GRAVY BISCUITS

½ pound lean bulk sausage
¼ cup butter or margarine
⅓ cup flour
3¼ cups milk

¼ teaspoon salt (optional)
½ teaspoon black pepper
pinch of Italian seasoning

- Brown sausage in a large skillet, cooking until it crumbles; drain and set aside.

- Melt butter in skillet; add flour, stirring until smooth. Cook about 1 minute, stirring constantly.

- Add milk gradually; bring to a boil over medium heat, stirring constantly until thickened.

- Stir in sausage and seasonings; cook until thoroughly heated, stirring constantly.

- Serve over split biscuits for a delicious breakfast.

Yield: 3 cups

Be careful with Italian seasoning as it can overpower gravy.

Demi Howard

SAUSAGE GRAVY

A family favorite for Christmas brunch!

1 pound pork sausage
   (sage or mild)
1 cup chopped onion

1-2 tablespoons minced bell pepper
⅔ cup flour
3½ cups milk

- Brown sausage in a large skillet; add onion and pepper and cook until soft.

- Push mixture to side of skillet and spoon out most of the grease.

- Sprinkle flour over mixture and stir constantly until lightly browned.

- Add milk slowly while stirring and continue cooking until mixture simmers and thickens. Add more milk if gravy becomes too thick.

- Keep warm and serve over hot baking powder biscuits.

Yield: 6 to 8 servings

Barbara Myers

NO-RISE ANGEL BISCUITS

They take their name from the heavenly light texture!

3 pounds self-rising flour   1 quart buttermilk
10 ounces shortening

- Combine flour and shortening in a mixer bowl; mix at low speed just until blended and mixture appears crumbly.
- Add buttermilk and mix until dry ingredients are barely moist.
- Transfer to work surface; pat or roll into ½-inch thick slab. Cut with a 2-inch cutter.
- Place biscuits 1½ inches apart on greased baking sheets.
- Bake at 425° for 10 minutes or until puffed and golden.

Yield: 50 biscuits

Add grated cheese, crumbled bacon or finely minced country ham.

Aimee Nelson

SAUSAGE PINWHEELS

2¼ cups biscuit baking mix   1 pound lean bulk sausage, pork,
⅔ cup milk   or venison
                                        8 ounces grated cheese (optional)

- Combine biscuit mix and milk; knead well. Turn dough onto a floured surface and roll into an 18x12-inch rectangle.
- Spread sausage evenly over dough and sprinkle with cheese; roll jelly-roll fashion from 12-inch side.
- Place on wax paper and refrigerate for 1 hour.
- Slice dough into ⅜-inch slices with serrated knife.
- Bake at 350° for 20 minutes.

Yield: 32 servings

Demi Howard

SAUSAGE GRITS

Great for brunch!

1 pound bulk sausage	3 cups hot cooked grits
2 cups grated cheddar cheese	3 eggs, beaten
3 tablespoons butter	1½ cups milk

- Cook sausage in a heavy skillet, stirring frequently, until brown. Drain and spoon into a greased 13x9x2-inch baking dish.
- Add cheese and butter to grits and stir until melted.
- Combine eggs and milk in a small bowl and stir into grits. Pour grits mixture over sausage.
- Bake at 350° for 1 hour. Serve hot.

Yield: 8 servings

May be assembled the night before and baked in the morning.

BAKED GARLIC CHEESE GRITS

1 cup grits	1 (6-ounce) roll garlic cheese
4 cups boiling water	2 eggs, beaten
1 teaspoon salt	½ cup milk
½ cup butter	

- Cook grits in water and salt until thickened. Add butter and cheese, mixing thoroughly until melted. Stir in eggs and milk.
- Pour into a greased 2-quart baking dish.
- Bake at 350° for 45 minutes.

Yield: 8 servings

Ellie Howard

OREGON HOMINY GRITS

3-4 cups cooked grits
1 cup sour cream
4 ounces green chilies, diced
1 pound Monterey Jack
  cheese, cubed

2 tablespoons Worcestershire sauce
2 eggs, beaten
salt and pepper to taste
Tabasco to taste
grated cheese (optional)

- Combine all ingredients and mix well.
- Pour into a greased baking dish and top with grated cheese, if desired.
- Bake at 350° for 45 minutes to 1 hour.

Yield: 6 servings

Rosa Blankin

JOSITA'S EGGS BENEDICT

4 rounds English muffins,
  buttered and lightly toasted
4 slices Canadian bacon,
  both sides browned

4 poached eggs
paprika for garnish

- Top muffin round with slice of bacon and poached egg.
- Prepare Mayonnaise Dressing. Spoon over eggs and sprinkle with paprika. Serve immediately.

MAYONNAISE DRESSING

¾ cup Hellmann's®
  real mayonnaise
⅓ cup milk

½ teaspoon salt
¼ teaspoon black pepper
1 tablespoon lemon juice

- Combine first 4 ingredients in top of a double boiler over simmering water.
- Cook 5 minutes to thicken; add lemon juice and stir. Be careful!! Will curdle if water boils!

Yield: 4 servings

Josita Montgomery

HOLIDAY STRATA

10 slices day old white bread,
  quartered
2 cups finely chopped ham
1½ cups grated sharp
  cheddar cheese
1½ cups finely diced red or
  green bell pepper

1 cup sliced fresh mushrooms
1 cup chopped green onion
9 eggs, beaten
4 cups milk
1½ teaspoons dry mustard
½ teaspoon black pepper
½ teaspoon paprika

- Arrange bread in overlapping rows in bottom of a 3-quart oblong baking dish; cover with ham and next 4 ingredients.

- Combine eggs and remaining ingredients; pour this mixture over ingredients in baking dish.

- Cover and refrigerate overnight.

- Bake at 350° for 40 to 45 minutes or until a knife comes out clean. Allow to stand 5 to 10 minutes before serving.

Yield: 12 to 16 servings

Ginny Cole

HAM, EGG, & CHEESE CUPS

12 slices bread, crusts removed
butter flavored non-stick
  cooking spray
1½ cups chopped cooked ham
6 eggs, lightly beaten

4 ounces processed cheese
  loaf, cubed
2 tablespoons finely
  chopped onion
2 tablespoons butter, melted

- Spray both sides of bread with cooking spray and press into muffin pans, forming 12 "cups".

- Bake at 350° for 15 minutes; set aside and cool.

- Combine ham, eggs, cheese, and onion. Scramble in butter in a large skillet over medium heat until eggs are done.

- Spoon into bread "cups" and serve immediately.

Yield: 12 servings

Demi Howard

EXCELLENT EGGS

A really great after-early-church dish!

12 slices white bread, divided	1 quart milk
½ cup grated cheddar cheese	1 teaspoon Worcestershire sauce
½ cup grated mozzarella cheese	1 teaspoon garlic salt
1 pound bulk pork sausage,	1 teaspoon paprika
browned and drained well	1 teaspoon dry mustard
butter	1 teaspoon nutmeg
5 eggs, slightly beaten	

- Place 6 slices of bread on bottom of a greased 13x9x2-inch baking dish.

- Cover with cheeses, sprinkle with sausage, and top with remaining 6 slices of bread and dot with butter.

- Combine eggs, milk, and remaining ingredients. Pour over bread mixture, cover and refrigerate overnight.

- Bake at 350° for 1 hour.

Yield: 8 to 10 servings

Delicious with baked apples.

Terry Girdauskas, Frances Guy,
Leslie Lang, Josita Montgomery, Joyce Person

CHEESE & EGG DISH

½ cup margarine	6 tablespoons flour
2 (16-ounce) cartons cottage cheese	½ pound processed cheese
6 eggs, beaten	loaf, cubed

- Melt margarine in a 13x9x2-inch baking dish.

- Combine remaining ingredients and pour into dish.

- Bake at 350° for 1 hour or until lightly browned.

Yield: 6 servings

May add a layer of thawed frozen spinach, which has had water squeezed out, between layers of cheese-egg mixture.

Gale Belser

'Pon Top Edisto

BISMARKS

A light and delicious way to begin Sunday!

½ cup butter
½ cup milk
½ cup flour

2 eggs
lemon juice to taste
powdered sugar for dusting

- Put butter in a heavy skillet or a shallow baking dish; place in oven set at 475°.

- Combine milk, flour, and eggs; mix lightly to form batter. Add batter to skillet when butter has melted and bake for 12 minutes. Remove from oven and place bismark on a plate.

- Pour a little of the butter on the pancake and squeeze on a little lemon juice. Roll up like a loose jelly roll and sprinkle with powdered sugar.

Yield: 1 bismark

Sprinkle with brown sugar, maple or fruit-flavored syrup, spread or fill with favorite fruit preserves or fresh berries or lightly sprinkle with Grand Marnier.

Laura Wimbish

CRISP WAFFLES

These are light and crispy!

2 cups biscuit baking mix
1 egg

½ cup oil
1⅓ cups club soda

- Mix all ingredients well.
- Bake in a hot waffle iron until done.

Yield: 4 servings

Makes great pancakes also.

Mary Alice Beck

34

OVERNIGHT REFRIGERATED WAFFLES WITH HEAVENLY HONEY

2½ cups warm water (100°)
2 packages active dry yeast
1 teaspoon sugar
⅔ cup powdered milk
3 cups all-purpose bread flour

⅓ cup salad oil
½ teaspoon baking soda
½ teaspoon salt
2 eggs

- Combine in a large bowl, water, yeast, and sugar. Rest for 5 minutes. Add powdered milk and next 5 ingredients. Beat until smooth.

- Cover bowl and refrigerate overnight.

- Heat 9-inch waffle iron to medium hot. Spray grid with non-stick cooking spray. Pour ¾ cup of batter into iron (adjust amount for different size irons). Cook until lightly browned.

- Prepare Heavenly Honey. Serve hot over waffles.

HEAVENLY HONEY

1 cup sugar
1 cup heavy cream

1 cup maple syrup

- Mix sugar and cream in a heavy saucepan; bring to a boil.

- Add syrup and blend well.

Yield: 4 servings

May make Heavenly Honey ahead of time. Let cool and refrigerate. Keeps for a week. Reheat when needed.

Mildred Ann Rodwell

BAHAMIAN BANANA PANCAKES

A real treat!

2 bananas, peeled and sliced
   crosswise into ¼-inch pieces
1¼ cups flour
2 tablespoons sugar
4 teaspoons baking powder
2 pinches of salt

2 eggs, separated
1 cup milk
2 tablespoons butter, melted
2 tablespoons vanilla
ground nutmeg for garnish
maple syrup

- Reserve ¼ of banana pieces.

- Sift together flour, sugar, baking powder, and salt; set aside.

- Beat egg yolks; mix in milk, butter, vanilla, and bananas. Combine mixtures and stir gently until moist and lumpy. Beat egg whites until stiff and fold gently into mixture.

- Drop by ¼ cup onto hot griddle; cook until underside is light brown; turn and cook other side. Place pancakes on a warm platter until all have been cooked.

- Garnish with reserved banana slices and nutmeg; top with maple syrup.

Yield: 12 to 15 pancakes

Dorothy Keach

HONEY-CINNAMON SYRUP

1½ cups sugar
½ cup brown sugar, firmly packed
1 cup water

1 cup honey
1½ teaspoons cinnamon
½ teaspoon maple flavoring

- Combine sugars and water in a saucepan.

- Bring mixture to a boil; remove from heat.

- Stir in remaining ingredients.

Yield: 2¾ cups

V. V. Thompson

SOUR CREAM BLUEBERRY PANCAKES

2 cups milk	2 tablespoons sugar
2 eggs	½ teaspoon salt
½ cup sour cream	4 tablespoons butter, melted
2 cups flour	1 teaspoon vanilla
2 tablespoons baking powder	1 cup blueberries

- Combine milk, eggs, and sour cream; beat well. Stir together flour, baking powder, sugar, and salt; add to egg mixture. Beat just until large lumps disappear; stir in butter and vanilla; fold in blueberries.

- Pour about ¼ cup batter on hot, lightly greased griddle for each pancake. When edges begin to look dry, turn pancakes. Watch carefully.

- Drizzle with syrup and enjoy!

Yield: 16 (4-inch) pancakes

John Kornegay

EASY POTATO-HAM PANCAKES

½ pound frozen hash brown potatoes, thawed	½ cup flour
	½ teaspoon salt
1 small bell pepper, finely chopped	½ teaspoon black pepper
	¼ teaspoon garlic powder
1 medium onion, finely chopped	¼ cup milk
½ cup cooked ham, chopped	¼ cup oil
1 egg, lightly beaten	

- Combine all ingredients, except oil. Shape into 4-inch patties.

- Heat oil in an electric skillet set at 375° or heat oil in a large heavy skillet over medium heat.

- Cook patties 3 to 4 minutes per side, or until golden. Drain on paper towels. Serve immediately.

Yield: 8 to 10 pancakes

Demi Howard

ELEGANT FRENCH TOAST

2 eggs	8 slices day-old French bread,
½ cup sugar	sliced ½-inch thick
1 cup milk	4 tablespoons butter, or as needed
1 teaspoon vanilla	powdered sugar
1 teaspoon grated lemon zest	grated nutmeg

- Beat eggs and sugar until thick. Stir in milk, vanilla, and lemon zest.

- Arrange bread in single layer in a shallow dish; pour egg mixture over and let stand 30 minutes.

- Heat butter in a large skillet; sauté bread until golden brown, about 6 minutes on each side.

- Arrange on a warm platter; sprinkle with powdered sugar and grated nutmeg. Yield: 4 servings

Aimee Kornegay Moore

CINNAMON STICKS

These are great and fun to make with children!

1 loaf white bread, crust removed	½ cup sugar
1 (8-ounce) package cream	1 egg yolk
cheese, softened	½ cup butter, melted

- Roll bread slices flat with a rolling pin.

- Mix cream cheese, sugar, and egg yolk; blend until smooth. Spread on bread slices. Roll each bread slice into a stick; roll sticks in butter until completely covered.

- Prepare cinnamon sugar mixture. Roll bread sticks in mixture until completely covered and dark. Freeze.

- Bake at 350° for 15 minutes.

CINNAMON-SUGAR MIXTURE

1½ cups sugar	6 tablespoons cinnamon

- Mix sugar and cinnamon.

May be kept in freezer for 2 months.

Clair Price

TUGGA'S STICKIES

2 tablespoons shortening	1½ boxes light brown sugar
2 cups self-rising flour, sifted	1 cup butter
¾ cup milk	2 tablespoons cinnamon

- Cut shortening into flour with pastry cutter. Add milk gradually and mix together.

- Knead dough briefly on floured board. Roll out dough to ¼-inch thick.

- Mix sugar, butter, and cinnamon. Spread sugar mixture on dough to the edges. Roll 1 side of dough to middle, then opposite side to the middle. Cut between the two rolls. Slice 1-inch thick and stand up in pan with seam side down with no space between them.

- Bake at 250° for 10 minutes, then 300° for 10 minutes and 350° for 40 minutes or until browned. Invert pan, separate while hot.

Careful! The sugar can burn fingers.

Jackie Adams

CECILIA'S CORN CAKES

2 eggs	½ teaspoon baking soda
1½ cups buttermilk	pinch of salt
1 cup cornmeal	1 tablespoon bacon grease, melted

- Beat eggs with buttermilk. Set aside. Mix cornmeal, baking soda, and salt.

- Combine buttermilk mixture with dry ingredients and add grease. Stir well.

- Heat skillet over medium heat; when skillet is hot, ladle batter by large spoonfuls into skillet. Flip over when done and cook other side.

Yield: 4 servings

Good with sorghum syrup.

Rosie Blankin

CHRISTMAS COFFEE CAKE

Delicious with morning coffee or afternoon tea!

½ cup butter, softened	1 teaspoon baking soda
1 cup sugar	1¼ teaspoons baking powder
2 eggs	1 cup sour cream
2 cups flour	1 teaspoon lemon juice (optional)
½ teaspoon salt	1½ teaspoons vanilla

- Cream butter and sugar; add eggs one at a time, while beating.

- Sift together flour, salt, soda, and baking powder; combine sour cream and lemon juice.

- Add dry ingredients alternately with sour cream mixture to egg mixture; stir in vanilla.

- Prepare topping; sprinkle a small amount of topping into a greased bundt pan. Pour half the batter into pan, sprinkle on half of topping; pour in remaining batter and sprinkle with remaining topping.

- Bake at 300° for about 1 hour.

TOPPING

½ cup sugar	½ cup ground nuts
2 teaspoons cinnamon	

- Mix all ingredients well.

  Yield: 12 to 16 servings

Josita Montgomery
Aimee Kornegay Nelson

COFFEE CAKE

1 box yellow cake mix	1 cup brown sugar
¾ cup vegetable oil	3 teaspoons cinnamon
4 eggs	1½ cups raisins (optional)
1 teaspoon vanilla	1 cup chopped nuts (optional)
1 cup sour cream	

- Combine cake mix and next 4 ingredients; pour into a greased 13x9x2-inch baking pan.
- Combine sugar, cinnamon, raisins, and nuts; sprinkle over cake batter and swirl with a fork.
- Bake at 325° for 40 to 50 minutes.
- Prepare icing. Pour over hot cake.

ICING

2 cups powdered sugar	4 tablespoons milk
1 teaspoon vanilla	

- Combine ingredients.

Yield: 12 to 16 servings

Aimee Kornegay Moore
V.V. Thompson

SUNSHINE COFFEE CAKE

1 box lemon cake mix
1 small box instant lemon pudding
4 eggs
½ cup vegetable oil

1 cup sour cream
½ cup sugar
¾ cup chopped nuts (optional)
1 teaspoon cinnamon

- Combine cake mix and next 4 ingredients and beat 4 minutes.

- Combine sugar, nuts, and cinnamon. Set aside.

- Pour half of cake batter into a greased 13x9x2-inch glass dish and top with half of sugar mixture. Repeat layers of batter and sugar mixture; swirl with knife to mix.

- Bake at 350° for 30 minutes.

  Yield: 12 servings

  This cake freezes well.

Josita Montgomery

Substitute yellow butter cake mix for lemon cake mix, French vanilla pudding for instant lemon pudding, and ½ cup butter for vegetable oil. Combine ¾ cup sugar and 4 tablespoons cinnamon for filling. Bake at 325° in a 10-inch tube pan for 45 minutes. Turn oven off; leave cake in oven for 15 minutes.

Madeline Huffines

APPETIZERS
&
BEVERAGES

'Pon Top Edisto

APPETIZERS

Crab Mousse
Smoked Oyster Roll
Crab, Cream Cheese, & Chili Sauce
Shrimp Mousse
"Edisto Creek" Shrimp Spread
∝ Shrimp Deviled Eggs
Smoked Fish Pâté
Pickled Shrimp
Marinated Shrimp
Cheese Ring
Smoked Salmon Ball
Pepperoni Cheese Ball
∝ Colony House Cheese
"Win Schular" Cheese Spread
Ripe Olive Spread
Spinach Dip
Jezebel Sauce
Chipped Beef Dip
Hidden Treasures
"Crickaway" Crab Grass
Ebby & Mary's "Edisto Crab" Edibles
Hot Crab Cheese Dip
∝ Cheese Buttons
Cheese Melts
Aunt Margaret's Blue Cheese
    Pull Aparts
Hot Mexican Dip
Cocktail Meatballs
Water Chestnuts with Bacon

Pinky Winks
Hot Spinach Dip
Spinach Balls
∝ Spinach Brownies
Artichoke Nibbles
Mushroom Squares
Pearl's Cheese Wafers
∝ Aunt Martha's Cheese Squares
Ham Delights
Lowcountry Boiled Peanuts

BEVERAGES

Friendship Tea
Granny's Mint Tea
Almond Tea
Back Porch Lemonade
Jiffy Lemonade Syrup
Hot Spiced Apple Cider
Hot Cranberry Juice
Wedding Punch
Bermuda Rum Swizzle
Fish House Punch
Bloody Marys
Cappucino Grand
Plantation Eggnog
Ever-Ready Daiquiri
Mimosa
Mint Julep

"Oh give thanks to the Lord, for He is good;
for His loving kindness is everlasting…
He has satisfied the thirsty soul,
and the hungry soul He has filled
with what is good."

Psalm 107:1, 9

44

CRAB MOUSSE

A delectable delight!

1 can cream of mushroom soup
1 envelope gelatin (dissolved in
   1 tablespoon water)
1 (8-ounce) package cream cheese
1 cup finely chopped celery

2 green onions, minced
1 cup mayonnaise
juice of ½ lemon
1 pound crabmeat

- Heat soup, add gelatin mixture; remove from heat, add cream cheese, and blend well. Add remaining ingredients and mix well.
- Pour into 2 greased 4-cup molds; refrigerate overnight.
- Serve with cucumber slices on round buttery crackers.

Yield: 3½ cups

May be molded in a loaf pan and sliced for a luncheon.

Judie Nye

SMOKED OYSTER ROLL

Easy and very good!

1 (8-ounce) package cream
   cheese, softened
2 tablespoons mayonnaise
2 teaspoons Worcestershire sauce

garlic juice to taste
onion juice to taste
1 can smoked oysters
chopped parsley for garnish

- Combine cheese and next 4 ingredients; mix well and spread on wax paper in a ½-inch thick rectangle.
- Place smoked oysters on top of mixture and roll in jelly roll fashion.
- Refrigerate for 24 hours.
- Roll in chopped parsley and serve with crackers.

Yield: 1 roll

CRAB, CREAM CHEESE, & CHILI SAUCE

An elegant appetizer to begin an evening!

1 (8-ounce) package cream
    cheese, softened
1 cup bottled chili sauce
1 teaspoon Worcestershire sauce
2 teaspoons lemon juice
¼ teaspoon chopped parsley

1 teaspoon chopped chives
1 teaspoon horseradish
¼ teaspoon Tabasco
1 teaspoon salt
½ pound white crabmeat
parsley for garnish

- Spread cream cheese on a serving plate.

- Combine chili sauce and next 7 ingredients.

- Cover cream cheese with sauce; top with crabmeat.

- Garnish with parsley and serve with crackers.

  Yield: 2½ cups

Gale Belser

SHRIMP MOUSSE

1½ tablespoons gelatin
¼ cup water
1 can tomato soup
3 (3-ounce) packages
    cream cheese
1 cup mayonnaise

¾ cup finely chopped celery
¾ cup chopped scallions
½ pound shrimp, cooked,
    peeled, and chopped
salt and pepper to taste

- Dissolve gelatin in water; bring soup to a boil, add cheese, and stir until dissolved. Add gelatin and cool.

- Add mayonnaise, celery, and scallions; mix well.

- Refrigerate to thicken. Pour into mold in layers with shrimp in between.

- Refrigerate overnight. Unmold and serve with crackers.

  Yield: 6 cups

Frances Leitner

Appetizers & Beverages

EDISTO CREEK SHRIMP SPREAD

Always a big hit!

⅓ cup sour cream
12 ounces cream cheese, softened
¼ teaspoon garlic powder

¼ cup Major Grey's chutney
1 cup shrimp, cooked, peeled,
and chopped

- Place sour cream, cheese, garlic powder, and chutney in bowl of food processor; process until mixture is of spreading consistency. Be careful not to over process.

- Put cheese mixture in a bowl and stir in shrimp.

- Chill. Serve with crackers.

Yield: 2 cups

Van Leer Rowe

SHRIMP DEVILED EGGS ⤜

8 hard-boiled eggs
2 tablespoons mayonnaise
1 cup shrimp, cooked and
chopped
2 tablespoons minced celery

2 tablespoons minced onion
2 tablespoons sweet pickle relish
salt and pepper to taste
paprika for garnish

- Slice eggs in half lengthwise; remove yolks and mash.

- Combine yolks with mayonnaise and next 5 ingredients; mix well.

- Spoon into egg whites and sprinkle with paprika.

- Chill.

Yield: 16 servings

Sallie Fontaine
Tag Wylie

SMOKED FISH PÂTÉ

¾ pound smoked trout
4 ounces cream cheese, softened
1 shallot, minced
1 teaspoon Worcestershire sauce
⅓ cup sour cream
several dashes of Tabasco

mayonnaise to moisten
black pepper to taste
garlic powder to taste
1½ teaspoons Old Bay® seasoning
2 tablespoons lemon juice

- Combine trout and next 5 ingredients; blend well.

- Add mayonnaise until pâté is smooth; add remaining ingredients.

- Refrigerate overnight.

- Serve with bagel chips or assorted crackers.

  Yield: 2 cups

Mary Elliott Fersner

PICKLED SHRIMP

5 pounds shrimp, cooked
  and peeled
2 onions, thinly sliced in rings

2 lemons, thinly sliced
6 bay leaves

- Place layers of shrimp, onions, lemons, and bay leaves in a bowl. Repeat layers.

- Prepare pickling sauce. Pour sauce over layers and refrigerate overnight.

PICKLING SAUCE

2 cans tomato soup
1 cup vinegar
1½ cups oil
½ teaspoon paprika
1½ teaspoons red pepper

1 teaspoon dry mustard
1 teaspoon garlic powder
1 tablespoon Worcestershire
salt to taste

- Combine all ingredients; mix well.

  Yield: 30 servings for hors d'oeuvres

  Drain before serving. Serve with toothpicks and/or crackers.

Gale Belser

MARINATED SHRIMP

A favorite at parties!

3 pounds shrimp, cooked
   and peeled
1 large red onion, sliced
1 large bell pepper, sliced
1 cup vegetable oil
2 cups ketchup
1 cup cider vinegar
2 tablespoons sugar
2 tablespoons prepared mustard

2 tablespoons Worcestershire sauce
1 teaspoon seasoned salt
1 teaspoon black pepper
2 dashes of Tabasco
2 cloves garlic, minced
2 tablespoons lemon juice
2 tablespoons horseradish
2 tablespoons seafood seasoning

- Combine shrimp, onion, and bell pepper; set aside.

- Combine oil and remaining ingredients; pour over shrimp mixture.

- Place in a large covered container and refrigerate for 8 to 24 hours before serving.

Yield: 15 to 20 servings

Serve with a supply of wooden picks and crackers.

Annabelle Creech

CHEESE RING

This is great for a party!

1 pound sharp cheddar
   cheese, grated
1 cup chopped nuts
1 cup mayonnaise

1 large onion, grated
salt and pepper to taste
Worcestershire sauce to taste
strawberry preserves

- Combine cheese and next 5 ingredients; mold into a ring.

- Fill center with strawberry preserves and serve with crackers.

Yield: 30 servings

Frances Richardson

SMOKED SALMON BALL

1 (16-ounce) can salmon, drained, boned, and skin removed, OR 2 cups cooked fresh salmon
1 (8-ounce) package cream cheese, softened
1 tablespoon lemon juice
1 teaspoon prepared horseradish
¼ teaspoon salt
dash of Tabasco
¼-1 tablespoon liquid smoke
2 teaspoons finely chopped onion
3 tablespoons chopped parsley
½ cup chopped pecans

- Combine salmon and next 7 ingredients; blend well.
- Shape mixture into a ball and chill overnight.
- Combine parsley and nuts; cover ball with mixture.
- Serve with crackers.

  Yield: 25 to 30 servings

  This will freeze well.

  Bo Lachicotte
  Sarah R. Arnold

PEPPERONI CHEESE BALL

2 (8-ounce) packages cream cheese, softened
1 (8-ounce) can crushed pineapple, drained
3½ ounces pepperoni, finely chopped
2 tablespoons minced dried onion
1 tablespoon seasoned salt
¼ cup chopped bell pepper
1 cup chopped pecans, divided

- Combine all ingredients, reserving ¼ cup pecans; mix well and shape into a ball.
- Cover with remaining pecans and serve with crackers.

  Yield: 1 cheese ball

  Barbara Hood

COLONY HOUSE CHEESE

1 pound cheddar cheese, grated
2 teaspoons dry mustard
½ teaspoon Tabasco
1 teaspoon garlic powder
1 tablespoon Worcestershire
   sauce
1 ounce anchovy paste

1 teaspoon chicken base
1½ teaspoons yellow
   food coloring
⅔ cup sour cream
1 ounce sherry
6 ounces stale beer

- Combine all ingredients except beer; beat at medium speed for 7 minutes.
- Add beer and beat at high speed for 4 minutes.
- Serve with crackers.

Yield: 3 cups

Tag Wylie
Henrietta McWillie

"WIN SCHULAR" CHEESE SPREAD

1 pound processed cheese
½ pound sharp cheddar cheese
1 (3-ounce) package cream
   cheese, softened

1 cup butter, softened
3 tablespoons sour cream
⅓ cup horseradish

- Blend cheeses and butter in a saucepan over low heat, stirring until smooth.
- Add sour cream and horseradish; remove from heat and beat until smooth.
- Pour into crocks or sealable plastic containers.
- Refrigerate.

Yield: 3½ cups

Missy Camp

RIPE OLIVE SPREAD

1 (8-ounce) package cream
   cheese, softened
½ cup sour cream
½ pound bacon, cooked and
   crumbled

1 cup chopped ripe olives
1 tablespoon chopped chives
   or onions
2 teaspoons horseradish

- Beat cheese until fluffy; blend in sour cream.
- Add bacon, olives, chives, and horseradish; mix well.
- Refrigerate for several hours or overnight.
- Serve at room temperature with crackers.

Yield: 3 cups

Joan Foxworth

SPINACH DIP

1 (10-ounce) package frozen,
   chopped spinach
1 cup sour cream
1 cup mayonnaise
½ cup chopped fresh parsley

½ cup chopped green onion
1 teaspoon salt
½ teaspoon dill
juice of 1 lemon

- Thaw, drain, and blot spinach dry.
- Combine with remaining ingredients; mix well.
- Serve with potato chips or shredded wheat crackers.

Yield: 4 cups

Great for sandwich spread, too!

Elva Richards

JEZEBEL SAUCE

1 (8-ounce) jar pineapple
  preserves
1 (8-ounce) jar apple jelly

1 tablespoon mustard
1 (5-ounce) jar horseradish
1 (8-ounce) package cream cheese

- Combine preserves, jelly, mustard, and horseradish; mix well.
- Spread sauce over block of cream cheese and serve with crackers.

Yield: 3 cups

This sauce keeps indefinitely in the refrigerator in a covered container.

Randolph Berretta
Linda Dennis

CHIPPED BEEF DIP

1 (8-ounce) package cream cheese
2 tablespoons milk
  (or more to thin)
1 (3-ounce) jar chipped beef, cut
  into small pieces
3 tablespoons chopped bell pepper
2 tablespoons minced onion
½ teaspoon garlic powder

¼ teaspoon black pepper
½ cup sour cream
1 tablespoon horseradish
  (optional)
2 tablespoons butter
½ cup chopped pecans
¼ teaspoon salt (optional)

- Soften cream cheese with milk in microwave and blend well.
- Add to cheese mixture next 7 ingredients; blend well and chill overnight.
- Bring dip to room temperature before serving.
- Sauté pecans in butter with salt until golden brown; spread on top of cheese mixture and serve with crackers.

Yield: 2 cups

Joan Foxworth

53

HIDDEN TREASURES

2 cups mayonnaise
½ cup horseradish, drained
2 tablespoons dry mustard
2 teaspoons lemon juice
½ teaspoon salt
1 pound shrimp, cooked
   and peeled
1 (6-ounce) can ripe olives,
   drained
1 (6-ounce) can whole
   mushrooms, drained
1 (8-ounce) can water chestnuts,
   drained
1 basket small cherry tomatoes
½ head cauliflower, cut into
   bite-size pieces

- Combine mayonnaise and next 4 ingredients; mix well.

- Add shrimp, olives, mushrooms, and water chestnuts to mayonnaise mixture; refrigerate overnight.

- Add tomatoes and cauliflower just before serving. Toss.

- Serve in a shallow bowl with picks.

   Yield: 10 to 12 servings

Helen Coker

"CRICKAWAY" CRAB GRASS

Very easy and delicious.

½ cup butter, melted
½ cup chopped onion
1 (10-ounce) package frozen
   chopped spinach, cooked
   and drained
1 cup crabmeat
¾ cup Parmesan cheese

- Sauté onion in butter until soft; add spinach, crab, and cheese. Heat thoroughly.

- Serve in a chafing dish with shredded wheat crackers.

   Yield: 3½ cups

Aimee Kornegay

EBBY & MARY'S "EDISTO CRAB" EDIBLES

A quick, easy, and very tasty hors d'oeuvre.

1 jar sharp Old English cheese
½ cup butter, softened
1½ tablespoons mayonnaise
1 teaspoon garlic salt
1½ teaspoons seasoned salt

red pepper to taste
½ pound crabmeat
6 English muffins, toasted
  after split

- Combine cheese and next 5 ingredients; mix well. Fold in crabmeat.
- Spread mixture on muffin halves; cut each into 6 wedges.
- Broil for 3 to 5 minutes.

Yield: 72 wedges

Freezes well. Just thaw and broil.

Mary Crawford
Ebby Hatch

HOT CRAB CHEESE DIP

An excellent quick or do-ahead appetizer!

1 (8-ounce) package cream cheese
1 pound crabmeat
1 teaspoon onion salt
½ teaspoon garlic powder
red pepper to taste

1 tablespoon Worcestershire sauce
1 (4-ounce) can mushrooms,
  stem and pieces, drained
dash of sherry
1 cup Hellmann's® mayonnaise

- Melt cream cheese in top of a double boiler; add remaining ingredients and stir until thoroughly heated.
- Serve in a chafing dish with toast points or crackers.

Yield: 4 cups

Van Leer Rowe

CHEESE BUTTONS

1 cup margarine, softened
2 cups self-rising flour, sifted
1 tablespoon Worcestershire sauce
2 cups grated sharp cheese

2 cups rice crispies
½ teaspoon red pepper or to taste
salt

- Combine margarine and remaining ingredients; mix thoroughly.

- Roll into marble-size balls; place on baking sheets and flatten (quarter-size) with a fork.

- Bake at 325° for 18 minutes until light tan; sprinkle with salt while hot.

Yield: 100 buttons

Gale Belser

CHEESE MELTS

A little messy, but good!

1 egg
1 cup butter, softened
¼ onion, grated
1 pound sharp cheese, grated

1 teaspoon prepared mustard
½ teaspoon red pepper
16-20 slices white bread

- Combine egg and next 5 ingredients; mix well.

- Spread on 8 to 10 slices of bread; cover with remaining slices and spread mixture on top; remove crust.

- Freeze on baking sheets; cut into 8 sections each.

- Bake at 350° for 5 to 8 minutes; serve hot.

Yield: 64 to 80 servings

Helen Coker

AUNT MARGARET'S BLUE CHEESE PULL APARTS

Everyone loves these, especially men.

1 (12-ounce) package
refrigerator biscuits
½ cup butter or margarine, melted

1 (4-ounce) package crumbled
blue cheese

- Cut each biscuit into quarters; place in a quiche dish.

- Combine butter and blue cheese; mix well and spoon over biscuits.

- Bake at 350° for 20 minutes.

- Serve with cocktail forks to pull apart.

  Yield: 40 bite-size pieces

Judie Nye

HOT MEXICAN DIP

1 (8-ounce) package cream
cheese, softened
1 (15½-ounce) can Mexican style
chili beans, partially drained

1 medium size red onion, chopped
1 (14-ounce) can green chili
peppers, chopped
8 ounces cheddar cheese, grated

- Spread cream cheese in the bottom of a 9-inch pie plate. Layer chili beans, onion, chili peppers, and cheddar cheese.

- Bake at 350° for 30 minutes. Serve immediately with tortilla chips.

  Yield: 10 to 12 servings

Barbara Hamlen

COCKTAIL MEATBALLS

2 pounds lean ground beef
1 cup corn flake crumbs
⅓ cup chopped parsley
2 eggs
¼ teaspoon black pepper

½ teaspoon garlic powder
2 tablespoons soy sauce
2 tablespoons minced onion
⅓ cup ketchup

- Combine all ingredients; blend well.

- Form into small balls; place in a flat baking pan.

- Prepare sauce. Pour sauce over meatballs.

- Bake at 350° for 30 minutes.

SAUCE

1 can jellied cranberry sauce
1 (12-ounce) bottle chili sauce

2 tablespoons brown sugar
1 tablespoon lemon juice

- Combine all ingredients in a sauce pan; cook until smooth, stirring occasionally.

If you are lazy like I am, you may buy frozen meatballs and warm them in the sauce. They are good, too!

Joan Foxworth

WATER CHESTNUTS WITH BACON

½ pound of bacon
1 (6-ounce) can water chestnuts
20 toothpicks

1 tablespoon soy sauce
1 tablespoon dry sherry

- Wrap ½ slice bacon around each water chestnut; fasten with toothpicks.

- Place in a baking dish and brush with mixture of soy sauce and sherry.

- Bake at 350° for 15 to 20 minutes.

Yield: 20 hors d'oeuvres

Ellie Howard

PINKY WINKS

1 pound ground beef, cooked
and drained
1 pound hot sausage, cooked
and drained
1 pound processed cheese
loaf, cubed

½ teaspoon garlic powder
½ teaspoon oregano
½ teaspoon Worcestershire sauce
2 loaves party rye bread

- Combine meats, cheese, and seasonings in a saucepan; heat until cheese melts.
- Spread mixture on bread; place on a baking sheet and freeze.
- Bake at 350° for 15 minutes or until bubbly.

Yield: 40 hors d'oeuvres

Jane Curtan

*1 pound sausage (hot or mild or ½ each), 1 pound cheese
(any kind, cubed), 1 teaspoon garlic salt, and 1 teaspoon
Worcestershire sauce.*

Naomi Irwin

HOT SPINACH DIP

1 (8-ounce) package frozen
chopped spinach, thawed
and drained well
1 (8-ounce) package cream
cheese, softened
1 (8-ounce) package Monterey
jack cheese, grated and
softened

⅓ cup half-and-half
2 tomatoes, seeded and chopped
¾ cup chopped onion
1 tablespoon chopped jalapeño
pepper
dash of Tabasco

- Combine all ingredients; mix well and pour into a casserole dish.
- Bake at 400° for 20 to 25 minutes.
- Serve with tortilla chips.

Yield: 4 cups

Mary Ann Heath

SPINACH BALLS

2 (10-ounce) packages frozen
   chopped spinach, cooked
   and drained well
1 (6-ounce) package prepared
   stuffing mix, including
   herb packet

1 cup Parmesan cheese
½ cup plus 2 tablespoons
   butter, softened
6 eggs, slightly beaten
salt and pepper to taste

- Combine spinach and remaining ingredients; mix well.

- Form into bite-size balls; freeze on baking sheet and transfer to freezer bags when firm. Thaw before baking.

- Bake at 350° for 10 to 15 minutes.

Choose herb seasoned stuffing mix to your taste.

Judie Nye

SPINACH BROWNIES

1 cup flour
1 teaspoon salt
1 teaspoon baking powder
2 eggs, beaten
1 cup milk

¼ cup margarine, melted
½ cup chopped onion
1 pound cheddar cheese, grated
1 package frozen chopped spinach,
   thawed and well drained

- Sift together flour, salt, and baking powder.

- Add eggs, milk, and margarine; stir well.

- Add onion, cheese, and spinach; mix well. Spread into a 13x9x2-inch baking pan.

- Bake at 350° for 35 minutes.

- Cut into squares and serve.

Yield: 24 servings (2x2-inch squares)

Johanne Albright

ARTICHOKE NIBBLES

Very tasty!

2 (6-ounce) jars marinated
  artichokes
1 small onion, chopped
1 clove garlic, minced
4 eggs, beaten
¼ cup fine bread crumbs
¼ teaspoon salt

⅛ teaspoon black pepper
⅛ teaspoon oregano
⅛ teaspoon Tabasco
½ pound sharp cheddar
  cheese, grated
2 tablespoons minced parsley

- Pour marinade from 1 jar artichokes into a sauté pan. Drain remaining artichokes; chop all artichokes. Set aside.

- Sauté onion and garlic for 5 minutes.

- Combine eggs, next 7 ingredients and artichokes; pour into a greased 11x7-inch baking pan.

- Bake at 350° for 30 minutes until set.

- Cool in pan. Cut into 1-inch squares. Serve cold or reheat at 325° for 10 to 12 minutes.

Yield: 6 dozen

Judie Nye

MUSHROOM SQUARES

Easy and very good!

2 cups biscuit baking mix	1 (3-ounce) package cream
½ cup butter, softened	cheese, softened
¼ cup boiling water	¼ cup Parmesan cheese

- Combine baking mix and butter; mix well. Add water to make dough.

- Grease a 13x9x2-inch pan and pat dough into bottom of pan. Spread cream cheese over dough.

- Prepare mushroom filling. Top cream cheese with mushroom mixture and sprinkle with Parmesan cheese.

- Bake at 350° for 20 to 25 minutes or until browned. Cut into 1½-inch squares when cool.

MUSHROOM FILLING

3 cups mushrooms, chopped	1 teaspoon Worcestershire sauce
¼ cup onion, chopped	2 tablespoons butter, melted

- Sauté mushrooms and onion with Worcestershire and butter for 10 minutes or until browned.

Yield: 54 squares

Mary Ella Hackett

PEARL'S CHEESE WAFERS

1 cup flour
2 cups grated cheddar cheese
½ cup butter or margarine,
   softened

½ teaspoon salt
¾ cup pecans, chopped

- Combine all ingredients and beat well.
- Divide dough in half and shape each half into a 10-inch roll.
- Slice into ¼-inch slices and place on greased cookie sheets.
- Bake at 350° for 15 minutes.

Yield: 6 dozen

Cheese rolls may be frozen; thaw at room temperature for 1½ hours, slice, and bake.

Denise Tutas

AUNT MARTHA'S CHEESE SQUARES ⊂✕

1 (6-ounce) package cream cheese
¾ pound cheddar cheese, grated
½ cup margarine
4 egg whites, stiffly beaten

1 loaf French bread, crust
   removed and cut into
   1-inch cubes

- Melt cheeses and margarine in top of a double boiler; when creamy fold in egg whites.
- Dip bread cubes (using long fork, small tongs or your fingers) into cheese mixture.
- Place on a foil lined baking sheet and freeze; remove from freezer and place in freezer bags until ready to use.
- Bake at 400° for 8 minutes on greased baking sheet.

Yield: 80 (1-inch) squares

Sarah Bolton

HAM DELIGHTS

Men, especially, enjoy these.

1 cup butter, softened	3 packages party rolls, split
3 tablespoons mustard	1 pound boiled ham, shredded
1 medium onion, minced	¾ pound Swiss cheese,
1 teaspoon Worcestershire sauce	thinly sliced
3 tablespoons poppy seeds	

- Combine butter and next 4 ingredients; spread both sides of party rolls with this creamed mixture.

- Place ham and cheese divided evenly over bottom halves of rolls; cover with tops of rolls. Wrap in tin foil.

- Bake at 400° for 10 minutes; cut into individual rolls to serve.

Yield: 60 servings

Freezes well.

Mary Crawford
Caroline Watson

LOWCOUNTRY BOILED PEANUTS

A traditional favorite at all outdoor parties!

4 pounds green peanuts in shell	6-10 tablespoons salt
6 quarts water	

- Place peanuts in a large stock pot with water and salt.

- Cover, bring to a boil, and boil slowly for 1½ to 2 hours.

- Test for doneness; peanuts will be soft.

- Allow to soak for 30 minutes. Drain.

Yield: 6 servings

May be frozen in plastic bags after cooling. Thaw and reheat by placing in microwave for 2 or 3 minutes.

Bob Dibble

FRIENDSHIP TEA

A great gift!

1 (18-ounce) jar orange flavored instant breakfast drink
1 cup sugar
½ cup pre-sweetened lemonade
½ cup instant tea

1 (3-ounce) package apricot flavored gelatin
2½ teaspoons ground cinnamon
1 teaspoon ground cloves

- Combine all ingredients in a large bowl and mix well.

- Store in an airtight container until ready to use.

- Serve by putting 1½ tablespoons of mixture in a teacup, fill with boiling water and stir.

Yield: 50 servings

V.V. Thompson

GRANNY'S MINT TEA

4 cups boiling hot water, divided
24 mint sprigs
5 family-size decaffeinated tea bags

2 cups sugar
1 cup lemon juice
12 cups cold water

- Steep together 2 cups boiling water, mint, and tea bags for 20 minutes in a heavy pitcher.

- Mix remaining 2 cups boiling water, sugar, and lemon juice in a 1 gallon container; stir until sugar is dissolved.

- Strain tea mixture and add to the container of sugar mixture.

- Fill gallon container to the top with cold water; mix well.

- Chill before serving.

Yield:1 gallon

If you choose to use caffeinated tea, use only 4 tea bags.

Mary Ann Heath

65

ALMOND TEA

3 tea bags
6 cups water
1 cup sugar

½ cup lemon juice
½ teaspoon vanilla
1 teaspoon almond extract

- Boil tea bags in 2 cups water for 5 minutes. Set aside.

- Boil sugar in 4 cups water for 5 minutes; combine with tea.

- Stir in lemon juice, vanilla, and almond extract. Serve hot.

  Yield: 8 cups

Aimee Nelson

BACK PORCH LEMONADE

A favorite summer cooler.

1¼ cups sugar
½ cup boiling water

1½ cups fresh lemon juice
4¼ cups cold water

- Combine sugar and boiling water, stirring until dissolved.

- Add lemon juice and cold water; mix well.

- Chill; serve over ice.

  Yield: 7½ cups

V.V. Thompson

JIFFY LEMONADE SYRUP

Great summer drink.

2 cups lemon juice   1½ cups sugar
4 teaspoons lemon zest

- Combine all ingredients and mix well.

- Pour ¼ cup of syrup into a tall glass and fill with ice cubes and water.

  Yield: 8 servings

                                                        Aimee Nelson

HOT SPICED APPLE CIDER

9 (46-ounce) cans apple juice   2 teaspoons allspice
2 teaspoons cinnamon   2 teaspoons ground cloves
2 teaspoons nutmeg

- Combine all ingredients in a large kettle. Heat thoroughly.

- Serve hot.

  Yield: 50 (1-cup) servings

                                                        Barbara Hood

"Keep us, O Lord,
as the apple of your eye."
Psalm 17:8

HOT CRANBERRY JUICE

2 quarts cranberry juice
1 quart water
2 quarts unsweetened
    pineapple juice

¾ cup brown sugar
2 cinnamon sticks
1 tablespoon whole cloves
1 tablespoon pickling spice

- Combine cranberry juice, water, and pineapple juice in the bottom of a 30-cup percolator.

- Place remaining ingredients in the basket.

- Perk; serve hot.

  Yield: 5 quarts

Gale Belser

WEDDING PUNCH

4 cups sugar
2 quarts water
1 (46-ounce) can pineapple juice
1 (12-ounce) can frozen
    orange juice

1 (12-ounce) can frozen lemonade
1 (8-ounce) bottle lemon juice
3 liters lemon-lime
    carbonated drink

- Combine sugar and water. Boil 10 minutes and let cool.

- Mix with all juices. Divide into 3 (1-gallon) plastic milk containers that have been cut around leaving the handle. Cover with foil and freeze.

- Remove from freezer about 1½ hours before serving time. Place 1 frozen slush mixture and 1 bottle of lemon-lime drink in a punch bowl.

- Mix into slush consistency and serve.

  Yield: 60 servings

Aimee Reese

BERMUDA RUM SWIZZLE

Do not drive! Watch the sunset on Edisto!

3 cups pineapple juice	¼ cup apricot brandy
2 cups orange juice	½ cup light rum
1 cup grapefruit juice	½ cup amber rum
2 tablespoons fresh lime juice	½ cup black rum
4 teaspoons simple syrup	¼ teaspoon Angostura bitters
(see below)	

- Mix liquids and simple syrup together in a large container. Pour into ice-filled glasses.

- Float slices of orange, lemon, lime, and maraschino cherries for color.

SIMPLE SYRUP

1 cup sugar   1 cup water

- Combine sugar and water; cook over low heat until clear.

- Boil a minute or so.

David Gibbons

FISH HOUSE PUNCH

Beware!

1¼ cups simple syrup	½ cup peach brandy
(see Bermuda Rum Swizzle)	½ cup Mount Gay rum
1¼ cups fresh lemon juice	1 cup brandy
2 cups water	3 cups club soda

- Combine all ingredients except club soda. Chill.

- Add club soda before serving.

- Serve in a punch bowl with cracked ice.

Yield: 20 servings

John Kornegay

BLOODY MARYS

1 (46-ounce) can tomato juice
6 tablespoons lime juice
4 tablespoons Worcestershire
   sauce

1 or 2 teaspoons horseradish
⅛ teaspoon Tabasco
salt and pepper to taste
1 pint vodka

- Mix all ingredients except vodka. Add vodka and pour into a 3-quart container.

- Pour over ice, add a twist of lime, and serve.

   Yield: 6 to 8 servings

   May be refrigerated for 1 month.

Mary Margaret Calk

CAPPUCINO GRAND

This is a wonderful after-dinner drink or dessert!

3 ounces kahula
2 ounces brandy
2 ounces Grand Marnier
2 heaping tablespoons dark
   brown sugar

8 cups freshly made strong
   hot expresso
2 cups heavy cream, warmed

- Heat kahula, brandy, Grand Marnier, and brown sugar in a saucepan.

- Add hot coffee and warm cream, stirring constantly until thoroughly heated.

   Yield: 8 to 10 servings

Brian Nelson

PLANTATION EGGNOG

A very old recipe and a Southern family tradition!

6 eggs, separated
1 cup sugar, divided
1½ cups bourbon or to taste

1 quart heavy cream, whipped
freshly ground nutmeg for garnish

- Beat egg yolks and ⅔ cup sugar, in a medium-size bowl, until mixture is lemon colored; slowly add bourbon, beating constantly.
- Beat egg whites and remaining sugar, in a large bowl until almost stiff.
- Fold bourbon mixture into egg whites; fold cream into egg mixture.
- Serve in punch cups with nutmeg sprinkled on top.

Yield: 20 servings

Eggnog tastes better if made the day before and refrigerated.

V.V. Thompson

EVER-READY DAIQUIRI

2 (6-ounce) cans frozen limeade
2 (6-ounce) cans frozen lemonade
2 (46-ounce) cans pineapple juice

1 quart light rum
mint sprigs for garnish

- Combine all ingredients except mint sprigs in a 1½ gallon freezer container. Mix until slushy.
- Store in freezer. Mixture will never freeze completely.
- Ladle into glasses when ready to serve and garnish with mint.

Yield: 18 to 20 servings

Freezing time: 2 days

Aimee Moore

MIMOSA

Great for bridal brunches and lunches!

1 fifth champagne, chilled	Strawberries for garnish
25 ounces orange juice, chilled	Mint sprigs for garnish

- Mix champagne and juice.
- Serve immediately.

  Yield: 1½ quarts

Judie Nye

MINT JULEP

1½ ounces mint syrup per serving (see below)	crushed ice
	mint sprigs
2 ounces bourbon per serving	

- Pour mint syrup and bourbon into each silver julep cup.
- Fill with crushed ice, add a straw, and garnish with mint sprigs.

MINT SYRUP

4 cups water	4 cups mint sprigs
2 cups sugar	

- Boil water and sugar over medium heat for ten minutes.
- Add mint sprigs and simmer 30 minutes.
- Set aside overnight. Strain.

  Yield: 25 to 30 servings

  To frost cup, after filling, dry outside and freeze at least one hour. Remove from freezer 30 minutes before serving.

Jesse T. Reese, III

SOUPS,
CHOWDERS,
STEWS

SOUPS, CHOWDERS, STEWS

Clam Chowder
∝ Clam Chowder
Edisto Seafood Chowder
Bobo's Shrimp & Corn Chowder
Kennebunkport Fish Chowder
Captain George's Fish Stew
Bobo's Red Chicken Stew
Old Fashioned Turkey Soup
Garbanzo Soup
Black Bean Soup
Cream of Mushroom Soup
∝ Vermont Ski Lodge Soup
Cold Cucumber Soup
Chicken Tarragon Soup
Pink's Fresh Okra Soup
Gazpacho
Baked Potato Soup
Dried-Tomato-Spinach Soup

"Beloved, I pray that in all respects
you may prosper
and be in good health,
just as your soul prospers."

III John 2

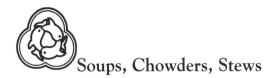

CLAM CHOWDER

⅛ pound bacon
1 pint freshly shucked clams,
   reserving juice
4 medium Irish potatoes

2 medium onions
2½ cups water
2 teaspoons ground allspice
salt and pepper to taste

- Fry bacon partially in a large, heavy bottom saucepan. Remove bacon (reserve drippings) and mince with clams, potatoes, and onions in food processor.

- Put in saucepan with bacon drippings; add water and clam juice. Bring to a boil and add allspice, salt, and pepper.

- Reduce heat and simmer 1 hour, stirring frequently to prevent sticking.

Yield: 1 quart

Aimee Kornegay

CLAM CHOWDER ⌖

½ pound lean salt pork, diced
2 medium onions, finely chopped
3 (16-ounce) cans tomatoes,
   chopped
1 quart clams, finely chopped or
   2 cans minced clams

1 cup diced potatoes
same amount milk as clams
1 teaspoon Worcestershire sauce
Tabasco to taste
NO SALT

- Brown salt pork in a large soup kettle; brown onions and add tomatoes. Bring to simmer point.

- Add clams and potatoes; continue simmering 30 minutes, stirring frequently.

- Add milk slowly and cook 30 minutes over low heat, stirring frequently. Add Tabasco. Do not let milk boil.

- Remember, NO SALT!

Yield: 2½ quarts

Wallace Trowell

EDISTO SEAFOOD CHOWDER

1 large onion, chopped
3 medium potatoes, cubed
2 carrots, sliced
2 teaspoons butter, melted
1 cup water
2 cups clams, minced
2 cups crabmeat
1½ cups creamed corn

1 cup kernel corn
1 bay leaf
½ teaspoon oregano
½ teaspoon parsley
½ teaspoon Tabasco
½ teaspoon salt
½ teaspoon black pepper
½ teaspoon sugar

- Sauté onion, potatoes, and carrots in butter in a large saucepan.

- Add water and simmer 20 minutes.

- Add remaining ingredients and simmer 20 minutes.

- Serve hot.

  Yield: 6 to 8 servings

Barbara Harmon

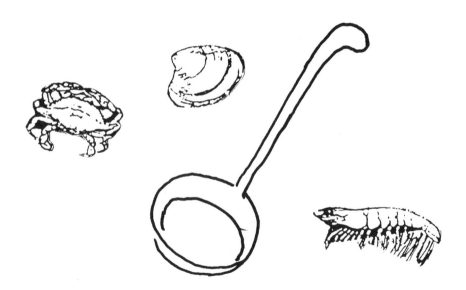

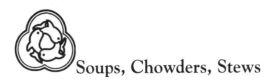

BOBO'S SHRIMP & CORN CHOWDER

Excellent!

6 strips bacon, diced
1 cup diced celery
1 cup diced yellow onion
½ cup diced bell pepper
4 cups corn kernels
4 cups small shrimp, peeled
1 pint strong shrimp broth
1 pint strong chicken broth

2 quarts heavy cream
2 quarts milk
1 tablespoon coarse ground
    black pepper
salt to taste
melted butter
flour

- Sauté bacon until it starts to brown; add celery, onion, and bell pepper and cook until wilted.

- Add corn and cook 3 minutes; add remaining ingredients except butter and flour.

- Bring almost to a boil, reduce heat.

- Combine butter and flour; whisk into chowder for desired consistency.

Yield: 12 to 16 servings

Robert E. "BoBo" Lee, The Pavilion Restaurant

KENNEBUNKPORT FISH CHOWDER

Try it, you'll like it!

¼ pound salt pork
   (more is better), diced
2 onions, sliced
4 cups potatoes, diced
1¾ cups water
2 pounds fish fillets
   (bass, flounder, or trout)

1 teaspoon salt
¼ teaspoon black pepper
2-3 cups milk
1 (12-ounce) can evaporated milk
1 small jar chutney

- Fry pork in a heavy kettle; remove and set aside when golden, reserving 3 tablespoons drippings.

- Sauté onions until yellowed; add potatoes and water to nearly cover.

- Place fish on top, sprinkle with seasonings; cover and bring to a boil. Turn heat to low; cook until potatoes are tender and fish flakes.

- Pour in milks and heat thoroughly; do not boil.

- Stir very gently to keep fish in large pieces.

- Reheat reserved pork, crumble, and sprinkle on top of each serving. Top with a spoonful of chutney.

Yield: 6 servings

Joan Foxworth

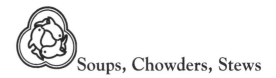

CAPTAIN GEORGE'S FISH STEW

Edisto's most famous stew.

2 jumbo onions, chopped	1 pint ketchup
2 pounds potatoes, diced	1 cup tomato juice
2 bell peppers, chopped	Old Bay seasoning to taste
2 cups chopped celery	salt and pepper to taste
1 pint crushed tomatoes	2½ pounds boned fish

- Combine vegetables in a large stock pot; cover with water and add seasonings.

- Bring to a boil and simmer over low heat until potatoes are tender.

- Boil fish in just enough water to cover until slightly cooked.

- Add fish broth to vegetable mixture; simmer until stew starts to foam. Do not boil.

- Ready to eat!

Yield: 1 to 1½ gallons

Bouchie Fontaine, Dock Side Restaurant

BOBO'S RED CHICKEN STEW

Marvelous!

1 large hen	1 (32-ounce) bottle ketchup
5 cups water	1 tablespoon black pepper
salt to taste	1 teaspoon cayenne pepper
4 strips bacon, diced	½ cup flour, mixed with water
3 large onions, sliced	6 hard-boiled eggs, sliced
3 cups reserved chicken broth	½ cup butter
½ (5-ounce) bottle	
Worcestershire sauce	

- Cover chicken with water in a large stock pot; salt to taste. Bring to a boil and simmer until tender. Drain, reserving broth. Set aside.

- Sauté bacon until fat has rendered; add onion and sauté until soft.

- Add 3 cups broth, Worcestershire, ketchup, and seasonings; bring to a boil and thicken with flour and water mixture.

- Bone chicken; cut into bite-size pieces. Add chicken pieces and hard-boiled eggs to broth mixture.

- Stir in butter just before serving; serve over fluffy white rice with a salad and hushpuppies.

Yield: 2 quarts

This stew seems to improve by resting for a day.

Robert E. "BoBo" Lee, The Pavilion Restaurant

"Now Jacob cooked a stew;
and Esau came from the field,
and he was weary.
And Esau said to Jacob,
Please feed me with that same red stew,
for I am weary."

Genesis 25:29, 30

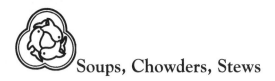

Soups, Chowders, Stews

OLD FASHIONED TURKEY SOUP

A wonderful after-Thanksgiving soup!

3 large onions, chopped	1 pint light cream or milk
3 stalks celery, chopped	salt and pepper to taste
3 medium carrots, chopped	2 cups turkey or chicken,
1 cup butter or margarine	cooked and diced
1½ cups flour	¼ cup cooked rice
3 quarts turkey or chicken broth	

- Cook vegetables in water to cover until tender; about 5 minutes. Set aside.

- Melt butter in a large soup kettle, blend in flour, and set aside.

- Combine broth and cream; heat. Add gradually to butter mixture, stirring to a smooth consistency.

- Add vegetables including water; stir and cook over low heat for 10 minutes. Season to taste.

- Add turkey and rice; cook until thoroughly heated.

Good served with wide Chinese noodles.

Joan Foxworth

GARBANZO SOUP

1 ham bone	1 can garbanzo peas
3 quarts water	1 pound frozen hot Italian
2 cups cubed ham	sausage, sliced
3 potatoes, cubed	¼ teaspoon saffron
2 onions, chopped	

- Cook ham bone in water for 2 hours.

- Add remaining ingredients and cook until potatoes are done, about 45 minutes.

Yield: 3 quarts

Caroline Crawford

81

BLACK BEAN SOUP

4 cups dried black beans
3 quarts water
1 quart chicken broth
¼ pound Canadian bacon, chopped
4 stalks celery, coarsely chopped

2 medium onions, coarsely chopped
salt and pepper to taste
¼ cup cream sherry (optional)
sour cream (optional)
yogurt (optional)

- Place beans in a large soup kettle and cover with water and broth. Soak, refrigerated, for 6 to 24 hours. Remove beans, reserving 1 cup beans and liquid.

- Purée remaining beans in food processor. Return all beans and liquid to pot; add bacon, celery, and onions.

- Simmer, uncovered, 2 to 3 hours, stirring frequently to prevent sticking. Add salt and pepper.

- Stir in sherry just before serving; garnish with sour cream or yogurt.

Yield: about 5 quarts

May be served over rice.

Walter Prause

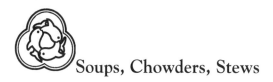

CREAM OF MUSHROOM SOUP

Delicious and easy to prepare.

12 ounces mushrooms, chopped	5 cups half-and-half
½ cup butter, melted	½ cup heavy cream
2 tablespoons flour	2 tablespoons cream sherry
1 cup chicken broth	salt and pepper to taste

- Sauté mushrooms in butter in a 3-quart saucepan until tender. Blend in flour and cook 1 minute. Add chicken broth and bring to a boil.

- Add half-and-half gradually, stirring constantly. Add heavy cream. Stir until well blended. Bring to a boil. Reduce heat and simmer 5 minutes or until slightly thickened.

- Add sherry and season with salt and pepper.

Yield: 6 cups

This makes a wonderful first course.

Billy Hiott

VERMONT SKI LODGE SOUP ⊂✕

This hearty soup is great on a chilly day!

2 pounds bulk sausage, browned and drained well	1 large bell pepper, chopped fine
4 (16-ounce) cans tomatoes, chopped	4 cans red kidney beans with juice
	4 cans water (tomato can)
3 medium onions, chopped	2 bay leaves
2 teaspoons seasoned salt	1 teaspoon garlic salt
¼ teaspoon black pepper	½ cup barley or rice

- Combine all ingredients in a large soup kettle.

- Simmer, covered, 2 hours or longer.

Yield: 16 to 20 servings

Maria Temple

COLD CUCUMBER SOUP

So-o-o good and cool!

5 cucumbers, peeled, seeded, and diced	1½ teaspoons salt
1 medium onion, chopped	1½ cups chicken broth (fresh, canned, or bouillon)
2 tablespoons chopped celery leaves	4 tablespoons butter or margarine
2 tablespoons chopped parsley	4 tablespoons flour
	1½ cups half-and-half

- Simmer cucumbers and next 5 ingredients in a saucepan for 30 minutes.

- Melt butter in another saucepan and blend in flour; add half-and-half and beat with a wire whisk; stir until thick and set aside.

- Purée cucumber mixture in food processor and add to sauce; stir until well blended.

- Refrigerate overnight. Garnish with parsley, chives, or a slice of cucumber.

Yield: 6 servings

Joan Foxworth

CHICKEN TARRAGON SOUP

½ cup celery, chopped	1 tablespoon tarragon leaves, dried and crumbled
½ cup onion, chopped	
¼ cup butter	1 cup cooked rice
⅓ cup flour	1 cup cooked chicken, diced
5 cups chicken broth	salt and pepper to taste
3 cups light cream	

- Sauté celery and onion in butter over low heat until transparent; blend in flour and cook 3 minutes.

- Stir in chicken broth, cream, and tarragon; cook over low heat 15 minutes, stirring occasionally. Do NOT allow mixture to boil.

- Add rice and chicken to soup; heat 5 minutes.

Yield: 2½ quarts

Jan Zehr

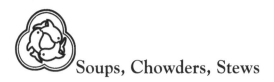

PINK'S FRESH OKRA SOUP

Best made with George and Pink's vegetables.

2 pounds okra, sliced
2 medium onions, chopped
3 tablespoons oil
6 vine ripe tomatoes, peeled
  and chopped
1 (8-ounce) can tomato sauce

1 medium bell pepper, chopped
1 ham bone, or ¼ pound
  bacon, chopped
salt to taste
½ teaspoon black pepper

- Sauté okra and onions in oil 5 or 6 minutes; set aside.

- Combine tomatoes, tomato sauce, bell pepper, and ham bone in a large pot; simmer 20 minutes.

- Place okra and onions on top of tomato mixture, add salt and pepper. Cook 1½ hours over low heat.

Yield: 8 to 10 servings

Fluffy white rice and cornbread are great with this lowcountry favorite.

Pink Brown, George and Pink Farm

GAZPACHO

A great sippable summer first course while grilling!

2 large tomatoes, peeled and cored	⅓ cup balsamic vinegar
1 large cucumber, peeled	¼ cup olive oil
and seeded	¼ teaspoon Tabasco
1 medium onion, quartered	1½ teaspoons salt
½ bell pepper, halved	⅛ teaspoon black pepper
¼ cup chopped chives	sour cream for garnish
24 ounces tomato juice	chopped chives for garnish

- Chop tomatoes, cucumber, onion, and bell pepper in food processor, a small amount at a time with ¼ cup tomato juice, retaining some of the crunch of the vegetables.

- Whisk together the vinegar, oil, Tabasco, salt, pepper, and remaining tomato juice.

- Combine all ingredients and chill at least 4 hours or overnight.

- Garnish with sour cream and chives.

Yield: 2 quarts

Mary Elizabeth Boykin
Aimee Nelson

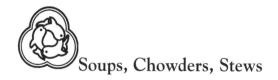

BAKED POTATO SOUP

Great for weekend guests for lunch or supper!

4 large baking potatoes, baked
⅔ cup butter or margarine
⅔ cup flour
6 cups milk
¾ teaspoon salt
½ teaspoon black pepper
4 green onions, chopped and divided

1¼ cups grated cheddar
   cheese, divided
12 slices bacon, cooked,
   crumbled, and divided
1 (8-ounce) carton sour cream
   or plain yogurt

- Cut potatoes in half, scoop out pulp, discard skins, and set aside.

- Melt butter in a heavy saucepan; add flour, stirring until smooth. Cook 1 minute, stirring constantly and gradually add milk. Cook over medium heat, stirring constantly, until thick and bubbly.

- Add potato pulp, salt, pepper, 2 tablespoons onion, ½ cup bacon, and 1 cup cheese. Cook until thoroughly heated and stir in sour cream. Add extra milk for desired consistency.

- Garnish with remaining onion, bacon, and cheese.

Yield: 10 cups

Van Leer Rowe

87

DRIED TOMATO-SPINACH SOUP

1 package dried tomatoes
2 cups boiling water
4 slices bacon
½ bag fresh spinach
1 can chicken broth

1 stalk celery, chopped
½ small onion, chopped
salt and pepper to taste
1 pint half-and-half

- Add tomatoes to water; allow to cool. Fry bacon, drain, and set aside. Dice tomatoes and reserve liquid.

- Pour ½ cup reserved liquid in a saucepan, add spinach, and boil 5 minutes. Chop spinach.

- Add chicken broth, celery, and onion to tomatoes and reserved liquid; boil 10 minutes. Add spinach, cooking liquid, crumbled bacon, salt, and pepper.

- Stir in half-and-half before serving; heat, but do not boil.

Yield: 6 to 8 servings

Floride Worthington

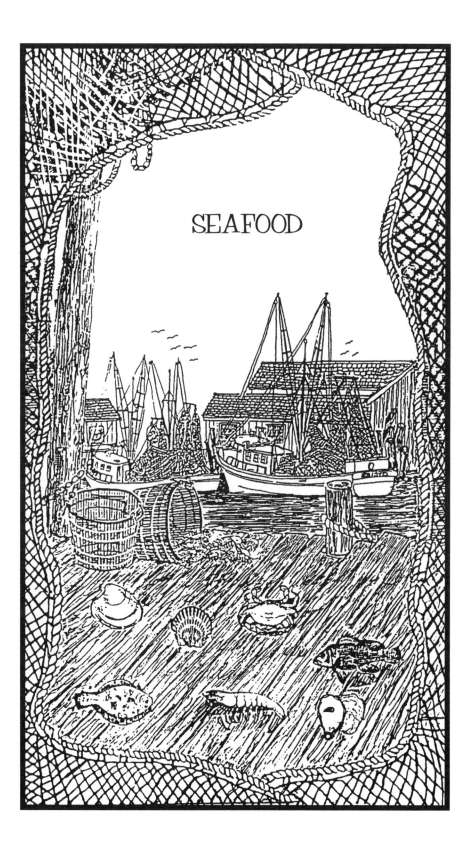

SEAFOOD

SEAFOOD

Edisto Island Clam Bake
Oyster Pie
Ginny's Oyster Pie
Philip's Oyster Skillet Roast
Drunken Scallops
Crab Soufflé
Divine Crab Cakes
Crab Oscar
Deviled Crab
Alamé
Bert's Own Deviled Crab
Crab Quiche
Crabmeat Fettuccine
Baltimore Crab Imperial
Crab Chantilly
Wine & Swiss Crab
Sautéed Garlic Crabs
Edisto Steamed Blue Crabs
∝ Scampi
∝ Crab & Shrimp Bake
Shrimp Pie
∝ Crab & Shrimp Casserole
Open-Faced Crab Sandwich

Shrimp Gravy
Sauce for Boiled Shrimp
Citrus Shrimp
Louis LeGarde Shrimp
Greek Shrimp
Artichoke Hearts & Shrimp
Sunnyside Shrimp Pie
"Cockle Shell" Shrimp
    in Sherry Sauce
Shrimp Casserole
Incredible Dolphin
Shrimp Casserole
Baked Fish Parmesan
Trout a la Jenifer
Fish Batter
Stuffed Trout or Flounder
Salmon Croquettes
Flounder Fantasy
Tomato-Mustard Sauce
Baked Whole Sea Bass
Tartar Sauce
Raspberry Salmon
Lemon Butter Sauce

"…When they got you upon the land,
they saw a charcoal fire already laid,
and fish placed on it,
and bread.
Jesus came and took the bread,
and gave them, and the fish likewise."
John 21:9, 13

EDISTO ISLAND CLAM BAKE

Let the men cook this one on the dock on the gas cooker!

24 cherry stone clams, in shell
1 chicken, cut into pieces
4 carrots, quartered
4 onions, quartered
4 Irish potatoes, peeled and
    quartered

4 sweet potatoes, peeled
    and quartered
1 bunch broccoli
6 ears corn, shucked
2 pounds shrimp, in shell

- Scrub clams until clean; place on bottom of a large Dutch oven.

- Place chicken pieces on top of clams; add carrots, onions, and potatoes.

- Pour about 5 cups of water over ingredients, cover, and steam 45 minutes, adding more water if necessary.

- Add broccoli and corn; steam 10 minutes. Add shrimp; steam 5 minutes. Serve with garlic French bread.

Yield: 6 to 8 servings

Buddy Rowe

OYSTER PIE

Excellent as a side dish with holiday ham or turkey!

1 box Oysterette crackers
1 pint oysters
4 eggs, beaten

¼ cup margarine
dash of black pepper
1½ cups milk

- Arrange layers of crackers, oysters, and eggs in a greased 1½-quart baking dish.

- Dot with margarine; add pepper and pour milk over all.

- Bake at 350° for 30 minutes or until browned.

Yield: 4 servings

Denise Tutas

GINNY'S OYSTER PIE

1 quart oysters, drained
 (standard or select)
1 (4-ounce) package fat free
 saltines, crushed and divided
juice of 1 large lemon
1 tablespoon dried parsley
1 tablespoon chives
1 tablespoon dried basil

1 tablespoon prepared horseradish
1 teaspoon minced ginger
1 teaspoon minced garlic
1 teaspoon seafood seasoning
red pepper to taste
butter flavoring to taste
paprika for garnish
lemon zest strips for garnish

- Set aside oysters. Cover bottom of a 9-inch pie plate with ½ of cracker crumbs.

- Combine lemon juice and next 9 ingredients; mix well.

- Place oysters over crackers; cover oysters with seasoning mixture and remaining cracker crumbs. Garnish with paprika and lemon zest strips.

- Bake, immediately, at 450° for 10 to 15 minutes or until lightly browned. You only want the oysters hot.

Yield: 4 servings

Do not assemble ahead of time. Takes about 15 minutes to prepare.

Virginia Guerard

PHILIP'S OYSTER SKILLET ROAST

Scrumptious!

2 dozen shucked oysters
2 cloves garlic, finely chopped
4 sprigs parsley, finely chopped
2 shallots, finely chopped

2 tablespoons butter, melted
1 tablespoon freshly squeezed
 lemon juice
salt to taste

- Combine all ingredients in a 6-inch skillet or baking dish.

- Bake at 400° until the edges of the oysters are curled and the liquid is bubbling. Serve with toasted French baguette.

Yield: 2 servings

Philip Bardin, The Old Post Office Restaurant

DRUNKEN SCALLOPS

2 pounds scallops
1 cup flour
2 tablespoons olive oil
2 tablespoons butter
½ cup chopped parsley
4 slices bacon, cooked
and crumbled

3 shallots, sliced
1 clove garlic, minced
1 teaspoon oregano
1 cup dry white wine
salt and pepper to taste

- Wash and thoroughly dry scallops; roll in flour to coat.

- Sauté all ingredients, except wine, in oil and butter, stirring to prevent sticking. Add more oil if needed. Remove scallops to a serving dish and keep warm.

- Pour wine into skillet, stirring to loosen all scallop bits, and boil until liquid reduces to half. Pour over scallops; season with salt and pepper. Serve with grits.

Yield: 4 servings

Aimee Kornegay

CRAB SOUFFLÉ

4 slices bread
milk
1 pound crabmeat
6 eggs, beaten
1 tablespoon seafood seasoning

½ cup butter or margarine, melted
2 tablespoons Worcestershire
sauce
2 tablespoons mayonnaise
1 tablespoon prepared mustard

- Soak bread in milk. Milk should cover bread.

- Mash bread in a medium-size bowl. Add remaining ingredients and beat until well blended. Pour into a greased 1-quart casserole.

- Bake at 350° for 1 hour or until firm and brown on top.

Yield: 4 servings

Jean R. Hiott

93

DIVINE CRAB CAKES

1 pound lump crabmeat
1 slice white bread, crusts
   removed and bread crumbled
1 egg, beaten
¼ cup mayonnaise
1 teaspoon dry mustard

1 teaspoon lemon juice
1 teaspoon Worcestershire sauce
½ teaspoon salt
¼ teaspoon black pepper
dry bread crumbs

- Combine crabmeat and bread very gently.

- Mix egg and next 6 ingredients until well blended. Add to crab mixture and mix lightly.

- Form into patties and roll in the dry bread crumbs. Refrigerate for 1 hour or longer.

- Cook in frying pan in just enough oil to prevent sticking; about 5 minutes on each side.

Yield: 6 to 8 servings

Crab cakes may be sprayed with vegetable cooking spray and baked at 400° for 5 minutes on each side on the lowest oven shelf.

Gale Belser

CRAB OSCAR

1 pound asparagus, cooked or
   1 (15-ounce) can asparagus,
   drained
1 pound crabmeat
1 cup sour cream
¼ cup mayonnaise

1 tablespoon lemon juice
¼ teaspoon salt
¼ teaspoon cayenne
¼ cup Parmesan cheese
   for garnish
paprika for garnish

- Arrange asparagus in a greased baking dish; top with crabmeat and set aside.

- Combine sour cream and next 4 ingredients in a saucepan; cook over low heat for 4 minutes. Pour over crabmeat, sprinkle with Parmesan and paprika.

- Bake at 350° for 20 minutes.

Yield: 4 to 6 servings

Jackie Houser

DEVILED CRAB

¼ cup butter, melted
2 tablespoons flour
1 cup milk
2 teaspoons lemon juice
1 teaspoon prepared mustard

1 tablespoon minced parsley
½ cup Italian bread crumbs
salt and pepper to taste
2 cups crabmeat
2 hard-boiled eggs, grated

- Combine butter and flour in a saucepan; gradually add milk, stirring over low heat until sauce is smooth and thickened.

- Add lemon juice and next 4 ingredients and blend well. Fold in crabmeat and eggs, gently. Put into a greased 2-quart baking dish.

- Bake at 400° for 30 minutes.

Yield: 6 servings

Sallie Fontaine

Add 1 teaspoon Worcestershire sauce, 2 tablespoons minced onion, and ½ teaspoon paprika.

Veda Godwin

ALAMÉ

1 small onion, chopped
¼ cup oil
2 tablespoons flour
1 teaspoon curry powder
1 teaspoon salt

1 can mushroom soup
¼ cup sliced mushrooms
3 cups cooked shrimp or crabmeat
¼ cup sherry
1 cup sour cream

- Brown onions in oil; add flour, curry, and salt, stirring until smooth.

- Add soup and mushrooms; bring to a boil.

- Reduce heat; add seafood, sherry, and sour cream. Do not boil! Serve over rice.

Yield: 6 servings

Jenks Mikell

BERT'S OWN DEVILED CRAB

Scrumptious!

1 pound crabmeat
½ medium bell pepper,
  finely chopped
1 medium onion, finely chopped
2 stalks celery, finely chopped
½ cup mayonnaise
¼ teaspoon seafood seasoning
½ cup butter, melted

2 eggs, slightly beaten
¼ cup cream or evaporated milk
2 tablespoons Worcestershire
  sauce
salt and pepper to taste
Tabasco to taste
bread or cracker crumbs
paprika

- Combine crabmeat and next 4 ingredients; mix seafood seasoning and butter; add to crab mixture.

- Combine eggs and next 4 ingredients; add to crab mixture.

- Add bread crumbs to make mixture soft but firm enough to pack into crab shells, cockle shells, or ramekins. Sprinkle paprika on top.

- Bake at 350° for 30 minutes or until brown on top. Do not overbake or they will dry out.

To make ahead, put crab mixture in shells, wrap individually, and freeze. Bake from freezer, allowing 15 minutes more baking time.

Yield: 4 to 6 servings

Bert Hatch

96

CRAB QUICHE

3 tablespoons butter, melted
3 tablespoons minced green onion
½ cup water
1 teaspoon salt
¼ teaspoon black pepper
½ pound crabmeat

3 tablespoons dry vermouth
3 eggs, beaten
1 cup half-and-half
1 tablespoon tomato paste
1 (9-inch) pie shell, partially baked
½ cup grated Swiss cheese

• Combine butter, onion, and water in a skillet; boil until water evaporates and onion is soft. Add salt, pepper, crabmeat, and vermouth. Bring to a boil.

• Combine eggs, cream, and tomato paste; stir into crab mixture. Pour into pie shell and sprinkle cheese on top.

• Bake at 375° for 25 to 30 minutes or until knife inserted in center comes out clean.

May be frozen and baked later.

Yield: 6 to 8 servings

Gale Belser

CRABMEAT FETTUCCINE

This one's very quick, very easy, and very good!

1 package Uncle Ben's Country
   Inn Recipes® Broccoli and
   White Cheddar Pasta
1 cup milk
1 cup water
½ pound Edisto blue crabmeat
   or more

1 (6-ounce) package frozen
   pea pods, thawed, drained,
   and cut in half diagonally
1 large tomato, seeded and chopped
¼ cup thinly sliced green onions

• Cook pasta according to package directions, using milk and water.

• Add remaining ingredients. Heat thoroughly, stirring occasionally, about 3 minutes.

Yield: 4 servings

A great lowfat meal, served with a green salad and crusty French bread.

Bert Hatch

BALTIMORE CRAB IMPERIAL

Delicious and elegant!

¼ cup unsalted butter, melted and divided
1 green onion, minced
2 tablespoons flour
⅛ teaspoon ground red pepper
⅛ teaspoon white pepper
⅛ teaspoon ground mace
½ cup milk

½ cup half-and-half
2 tablespoons dry sherry
½ cup mayonnaise
juice of ½ lemon
salt to taste
1 pound lump crabmeat
paprika for garnish

- Combine 2 tablespoons butter and onion in a heavy saucepan over medium heat; stir until lightly browned, 5 to 8 minutes.

- Stir in flour, peppers, and mace for 1 to 2 minutes; add milk, cream, and sherry; cook until thick and smooth, 3 to 4 minutes.

- Remove from heat; stir in mayonnaise, lemon juice, and salt. Set aside.

- Combine remaining 2 tablespoons butter and crab in a large, heavy skillet over medium heat; cook 1 minute and gently fold sauce into crab.

- Spoon mixture into a gratin dish or individual shells. May be prepared in advance to this point. Sprinkle with paprika.

- Bake at 350° for 12 to 15 minutes, or 20 to 25 minutes if prepared in advance.

Yield: 4 servings

Gale Belser

CRAB CHANTILLY

Exceptionally elegant!

2 tablespoons chopped green onion
2 tablespoons butter, melted
1 tablespoon flour
½ teaspoon salt
dash of cayenne
1 cup half-and-half
¼ cup salad dressing
(not mayonnaise)

1 pound lump crabmeat
sherry or vermouth (optional)
1 (10-ounce) package frozen
asparagus or 1 pound fresh
asparagus, cooked
¼ cup Parmesan cheese

- Sauté onion in butter until tender; blend in flour, salt, and cayenne. Add cream; cook, stirring constantly, until thickened. Remove from heat. Stir in salad dressing, crabmeat, and sherry.

- Arrange asparagus on a heatproof platter or in a 1½-quart baking dish. Spoon crab mixture over asparagus. Sprinkle with Parmesan.

- Broil, 4 inches from heat, for 3 or 4 minutes or until lightly browned.

May prepare ahead; Bake at 350° for 30 minutes or until lightly browned and bubbly.

Yield: 4 to 6 servings

Gale Belser

Thank you for the food we eat;
Thank you for the friends we meet;
Thank you for our work and play;
Thank you, God, for a happy day.
Amen

WINE & SWISS CRAB

Different and devilishly delicious!

6 slices firm white bread
1 cup dry white wine
⅓ cup plus 4 tablespoons butter,
  melted and divided
1 pound Edisto blue crabmeat
2 tablespoons flour

1 cup milk
2 cups grated Swiss cheese
2 egg yolks
1 teaspoon salt
¼ teaspoon black pepper
½ teaspoon paprika

- Soak bread in wine for 5 minutes; bread should be drenched but still keep its shape. Place in a greased 13x9x2-inch baking dish.

- Pour ⅓ cup butter over bread and cover with crabmeat.

- Blend 2 tablespoons butter and flour in a saucepan; gradually stir in milk. Cook over low heat, stirring constantly, until thick and smooth. Remove from heat.

- Add cheese and stir until melted. Beat in yolks, salt, pepper, and paprika. Spoon over crab mixture and drizzle with remaining butter.

- Bake at 400° for 10 to 15 minutes until top is browned and bubbly.

Yield: 6 servings

Bert Hatch

100

SAUTÉED GARLIC CRABS

This is an Edisto favorite!

14 live crabs
½ cup butter or margarine

4-5 cloves garlic, minced
Old Bay Seasoning® to taste

- Place crabs on ice to make them lethargic; clean crabs raw: break off claws but leave legs; break bodies in half.

- Melt butter and garlic in a 10-inch iron skillet over low heat; remove from heat and add 1 tablespoon Old Bay. Mix well.

- Place crab bodies on end with feelers up in skillet. Sprinkle seasonings over crabs. The more the spicier. Cover skillet with lid.

- Place skillet over high heat. Cook 5 minutes.

- Hold lid loosely over skillet and pour butter into a heat proof measuring cup. Return skillet to heat. Drizzle butter over crabs. Cover and cook 2 minutes. Repeat this process 2 additional times.

- The garlic butter will turn a golden brown and some crabs will be blackened. Not to worry! These are the best!

Yield: 14 crabs

Serve on newspaper; each person picks their own.

Annabelle Creech

EDISTO STEAMED BLUE CRABS

A great casual dinner for a crowd,
served with tossed salad and iced down beer!

12 ounces beer	Old Bay Seasoning® to taste
12 ounces water	12-24 live blue crabs
12 ounces White Vinegar	

- Pour liquids into a large stock pot to a depth of 1-inch.

- Place a rack in pot; layer crabs on rack, sprinkling each layer heavily with seasoning.

- Steam for 10 to 15 minutes or until crabs turn a deep bright red.

- Serve hot or cold.

  Yield: 4 crabs per person

  Fun to cook outside and serve on a newspaper covered table. Place crabs directly on newspaper and enjoy.

  Buddy Rowe

SCAMPI ⊂×

2 pounds shrimp, peeled	¾ teaspoon lemon pepper
⅓ cup olive oil or margarine	3 tablespoons lemon juice
½ cup dry sherry or vermouth	3 tablespoons chopped parsley
1 teaspoon garlic salt	

- Sauté shrimp in olive oil.

- Add sherry, garlic salt, lemon pepper, and lemon juice; simmer until liquid is almost absorbed.

- Sprinkle with parsley and stir gently to mix.

  Yield: 4 servings

  Amy Trowel

CRAB & SHRIMP BAKE ✕

An Edisto Island favorite!

2 cups lump crabmeat
2 cups shrimp, cooked and peeled
1 cup chopped celery
½ cup chopped onion
½ cup chopped bell pepper
¼ teaspoon salt

⅛ teaspoon black pepper
1 teaspoon Worcestershire sauce
2 tablespoons white wine
1 cup mayonnaise
potato chips, crumbled

- Combine all ingredients, except potato chips; mix well.
- Place in a greased baking dish; sprinkle with chips.
- Bake at 350° for 30 minutes.

Yield: 6 to 8 servings

Instead of potato chips, top with 1½ cups grated longhorn cheese or buttered bread crumbs.

Sallie Fontaine
Joyce Person

SHRIMP PIE

6 slices bacon, cut in pieces
2 large onions, chopped
1 large bell pepper, chopped
1 (16-ounce) can tomatoes
½ teaspoon salt
¼ teaspoon black pepper

1 teaspoon sugar
1 teaspoon Worcestershire sauce
5-6 slices bread, toasted
2 pounds shrimp, cooked
  and peeled
1 cup grated sharp cheese

- Sauté bacon, onions, and pepper; drain. Add tomatoes and next 4 ingredients and cook 10 minutes.
- Place toast in a greased shallow baking dish and cover with sauce. Place shrimp over sauce and sprinkle with cheese.
- Bake at 350° for 30 minutes or until bubbly.

Yield: 4 servings

Peg Stover

103

CRAB & SHRIMP CASSEROLE

"The best!"

1 chicken bouillon cube
¾ cup hot water
3 cups shredded white bread
1 cup chopped celery
1 cup chopped onion
½ cup chopped bell pepper
2 tablespoons butter, melted
1 cup mayonnaise
2 teaspoons dry mustard

2 tablespoons Worcestershire
   sauce
½ teaspoon curry powder
dash of mace
salt and pepper to taste
large dash of dry sherry
1 pound crabmeat
2 pounds shrimp, cooked,
   and peeled

- Dissolve bouillon cube in hot water. Pour over bread to soak.

- Sauté vegetables in butter.

- Combine mayonnaise and next 6 ingredients; mix well.

- Add crabmeat and shrimp.

- Combine all ingredients and place in a greased 3-quart glass casserole dish (13x9x2-inch) and refrigerate overnight.

- Remove from refrigerator and sprinkle with crushed round buttery crackers.

- Bake at 350° for 30 to 40 minutes, until hot and brown.

Yield: 10 to 12 servings

Gertrude Woods

OPEN-FACED CRAB SANDWICH

This is a great luncheon or Sunday supper sandwich.

4 slices pumpernickel bread
8 ounces fresh crabmeat
2 stalks celery, finely chopped
4 scallions, chopped
5-6 mushrooms, sliced

1 teaspoon caraway seeds
3-4 teaspoons mayonnaise
2-3 tablespoons sour cream
8 slices bacon, fried and drained
4 slices cheddar cheese

- Toast bread under broiler on one side only. Place toasted side down on a baking sheet.

- Combine crabmeat and next 6 ingredients.

- Spread mixture evenly on untoasted side of bread; top each serving with 2 slices of bacon and a slice of cheese.

- Broil until cheese melts and bubbles. It is not necessary that the other ingredients be hot through and through.

Yield: 4 servings

Ebby serves this with a simple salad, such as asparagus on lettuce leaves, with tomato wedges.

Bert Hatch

SHRIMP GRAVY

A lowcountry favorite!

5 slices bacon
1 bunch spring onions,
   including tops
4 cloves garlic, minced
1 bell pepper, chopped
1 tablespoon flour

1 (12-ounce) package
   mushrooms, sliced
1½ pounds shrimp, peeled
   and deveined
garlic salt to taste
black pepper to taste
3 cups cooked grits

- Fry bacon in a large skillet until crisp. Remove bacon and set aside. Pour off half of grease.

- Sauté onions, garlic, and bell pepper in remaining bacon grease on high heat. Sprinkle flour into mixture and blend well. Add mushrooms and shrimp. Cover and stir often until shrimp turn pink. Season with garlic salt and pepper.

- Serve over hot grits topped with crumbled bacon.

Yield: 4 to 6 servings

May substitute oysters for shrimp.

Tom Kapp

SAUCE FOR BOILED SHRIMP

Please measure carefully!

1 generous dollop Hellmann's®
mayonnaise — regular or
lowfat (regular preferred)
3-6 blobs ketchup
3-6 squirts Tabasco

½ teaspoon Worcestershire sauce
scrapings from the cut surface of
a small onion
seasoned salt

- Place mayonnaise in a small shallow dessert dish. Add ketchup and stir until smooth and a light salmon color.

- Add Tabasco and stir in well. Repeat with Worcestershire sauce.

- Scrape the cut surface of small onion onto the mixture until there are small droplets of onion juice and small fragments of onion on the surface. Mix.

- Sprinkle with seasoned salt; mix again.

Yield: Serves one to several, depending on time of day, meal at which offered, nature of the occasion at which served, size of guests, appetite of same and other miscellaneous factors.

Ingredients may be varied as the chef's imagination and sense of adventure dictates.

BOILED SHRIMP

shrimp   water
salt

- Shrimp should be boiled in salted water. Bring water to a rolling boil and add ½ to ¾ volume of shrimp to one volume of water.

- Allow to return to a rolling boil and empty into a colander to drain.

- May be eaten hot or cold.

Yield: Your choice

Freshly caught shrimp may be boiled with heads on, thus relieving you of the nuisance of heading them and adding to their flavor.

Curtis Worthington

CITRUS SHRIMP

A very casual dinner!

4 pounds raw shrimp
½ cup butter or margarine
garlic salt to taste

3-4 oranges, sliced
3-4 lemons, sliced

- Preheat broiler.

- Spread shrimp in broiler pan and dot with butter; sprinkle generously with garlic salt and cover with orange slices; then cover with lemon slices.

- Broil until shrimp turn pink, stirring often.

- Serve in the pan with a loaf of good soft bread for "sopping" the wonderful pan juices.

  Yield: 8 servings

Jackie Adams

LOUIS LEGARDE SHRIMP

Spicy and fun!

½ cup unsalted butter, melted
1 tablespoon minced garlic
½ teaspoon dried rosemary
½ teaspoon oregano
1 teaspoon cayenne

½ teaspoon black pepper
½ teaspoon thyme
1 pound large shrimp in shell
¼ cup white wine

- Combine butter and spices in a 10-inch skillet and heat.

- Add shrimp and wine; cook until shrimp turn pink, shaking pan, about 3 minutes.

- Serve with crusty French bread for dunking in sauce.

  Yield: 2 servings

Jan Rasmussen

GREEK SHRIMP

¼ cup olive oil
1 (8-ounce) can tomato sauce
1 can tomato soup
juice of large lemon
1 tablespoon Greek seasoning
2 cloves garlic, minced
1 tablespoon dried parsley

3 stalks celery with leaves, chopped
1 large onion, chopped
1 medium bell pepper, chopped
lemon zest to taste (optional)
1 small can sliced ripe olives
1½ pounds shrimp, peeled
4 ounces Feta cheese, crumbled

- Combine olive oil and next 9 ingredients in a large saucepan and simmer 1 hour, stirring occasionally.

- Grate lemon zest and add to sauce; add olives and shrimp.

- Cook until shrimp turn pink; serve over rice with crumbled cheese on top.

  Yield: 6 servings

Virginia Guerard

ARTICHOKE HEARTS & SHRIMP

2 cans artichoke hearts, drained
  and quartered
1½ pounds shrimp, cooked
  and peeled
1 (6-ounce) can button
  mushrooms, drained
3 tablespoons butter, melted
3 tablespoons flour
¾ teaspoon salt

¼ teaspoon black pepper
dash of cayenne
1 cup half-and-half
1 tablespoon Worcestershire
  sauce
½ cup dry sherry
¼ cup Parmesan cheese
paprika

- Layer artichokes in a greased, shallow baking dish. Layer shrimp and mushrooms on top.

- Combine butter and next 5 ingredients to make white sauce in a saucepan over medium heat; add Worcestershire sauce and sherry; blend well.

- Pour white sauce over shrimp; sprinkle with Parmesan and paprika.

- Bake at 375° for 20 minutes.

  Yield: 6 servings

Aimee Nelson

SUNNYSIDE SHRIMP PIE

1 pound shrimp, cooked and peeled
1 cup finely chopped bell pepper
1 cup finely chopped onion
1 cup finely chopped celery
2 hard-boiled eggs, finely chopped
juice of 2 lemons
¼ cup butter or margarine, melted
½ cup flour
½ teaspoon salt
1 pint milk
½ pound sharp cheddar
  cheese, grated
dash of A-1® sauce
dash of ketchup
½ cup bread crumbs

- Combine shrimp and next 5 ingredients. Set aside.

- Put butter in a heavy saucepan; add flour and salt. Stir until well blended over medium heat. Add milk, stirring constantly until sauce thickens. Stir in cheese, A-1 sauce, and enough ketchup to add color, if desired.

- Combine the mixtures and spoon into a greased baking dish; sprinkle bread crumbs on top.

- Bake at 350° for 30 minutes.

Yield: 4 to 6 servings

Gale Belser

"COCKLE SHELL" SHRIMP IN SHERRY SAUCE

Very rich and filling!

2 tablespoons butter, melted
1½ tablespoons flour
¾ cup milk
½ pound shrimp, cooked and peeled
¼ teaspoon salt

dash of black pepper
dash of paprika
2 tablespoons dry sherry
Parmesan cheese

- Combine butter and flour in a heavy saucepan over low heat, stirring until smooth. Cook 1 minute, stirring constantly.

- Add milk, gradually, and cook over medium heat until thickened and bubbly.

- Add shrimp and next 4 ingredients and stir well.

- Spoon into 2 (10-ounce) ramekins or large cockle shells; sprinkle each with Parmesan.

- Broil 3 or 4 inches from heat until cheese is lightly browned.

Yield: 2 servings

Can be multiplied ad infinitum.

Bert Hatch

SHRIMP CASSEROLE

2 cups shrimp, cooked and peeled
1 cup chopped celery
1 small onion, grated
2 cups cooked rice
3 hard-boiled eggs, chopped
½ cup slivered almonds, toasted

2 tablespoons lemon juice
1 can mushroom soup
¼ cup milk
¾ cup mayonnaise
salt and pepper to taste
potato chips, crushed

- Combine all ingredients, except potato chips; mix well and spoon into a greased 2-quart baking dish. Refrigerate overnight.

- Remove from refrigerator; sprinkle with crushed potato chips.

- Bake at 350° for 30 minutes or until hot throughout.

Yield: 4 to 6 servings

Tuna or chicken may be substituted for shrimp.

Barbara Hood

INCREDIBLE DOLPHIN

Definitely delicious!

1 pound dolphin filets,
    dark meat removed
5-6 tablespoons light corn syrup
2 cups milk

garlic powder to taste
seasoned salt to taste
cracker meal
½ cup butter, melted

- Cut filets into 2x¾-inch strips; combine syrup and milk, add filet strips and marinate 2 to 24 hours, covered and refrigerated.

- Place fish on wax paper to drip dry. Do not pat dry.

- Season lightly with garlic powder and seasoning salt and dredge fish in cracker meal.

- Sauté fish in butter until golden brown, about 5 minutes; turn and brown other side, about 5 minutes.

Yield: 2 servings

Fred Inman

SHRIMP CASSEROLE

4 slices bread, cubed
1 pound sharp cheddar
    cheese, grated
1 cup water
½ cup butter, divided
1 cup chopped onion
½ cup chopped bell pepper

1 cup chopped celery
2 pounds shrimp, cooked
    and peeled
1 egg, beaten
5-6 drops Tabasco
½ cup mayonnaise
crushed round buttery crackers

- Combine bread, cheese, and water in a large bowl; set aside.

- Sauté onion, pepper, and celery in ¼ cup butter until tender. Add shrimp.

- Add shrimp mixture, egg, Tabasco, and mayonnaise to bread/cheese mixture; blend well.

- Pour into a 3-quart casserole dish and top until crushed crackers and dot with remaining butter.

- Bake at 350° for 30 minutes or until well heated.

Yield: 8 to 10 servings

Joan Halliday

BAKED FISH PARMESAN

2 pounds fish (grouper, tile,
    flounder, etc.)
1 cup low fat sour cream
¼ cup Parmesan cheese
1 tablespoon lemon juice

1 tablespoon grated onion
¼ teaspoon salt
⅛ teaspoon Tabasco
chopped parsley for garnish

- Place fish in a well greased baking dish.

- Combine remaining ingredients and spread over fish.

- Bake at 350° for 25 to 30 minutes or until fish flakes.

Yield: 6 servings

Peg Stover

113

TROUT A LA JENIFER

Excellent and easy to prepare.

1 cup mushrooms, sliced	1 tablespoon olive oil
1 large sweet onion, sliced	1 cup Caesar salad dressing
pinch of sweet basil	4 filets of Trout
pinch of cayenne	Parmesan cheese
pinch of salt	1 cup chopped walnuts
2 tablespoons dry white vermouth	

- Sauté mushrooms and next 5 ingredients in olive oil until mushrooms and onion start to soften; remove from saucepan.

- Pour salad dressing into a bowl. Dip filets into dressing and place in a shallow baking dish.

- Cover with a medium coat of Parmesan; top with mushroom mixture, walnuts, and more cheese.

- Bake at 400° for 20 to 25 minutes.

Yield: 4 servings

As a leftover, break up fish and add to pasta.

Jenifer Lachicotte

FISH BATTER

This batter makes a good catch even better!

1 cup flour	1 tablespoon oil
1 teaspoon salt	1 egg
2 teaspoons baking powder	6 ounces beer

- Combine all ingredients and mix well. Dip prepared fish in the batter and fry.

Yield: 2 cups

Cantey Richardson

STUFFED TROUT OR FLOUNDER

1 cup minced onion	1 cup dry white wine
1½ cups minced celery	½ cup chopped, cooked shrimp
½ cup minced shallots	½ cup lump crabmeat
3 cloves garlic, minced	½ bunch parsley, chopped
1 cup margarine, melted	2½ cups bread crumbs
2 tablespoons flour	salt and pepper to taste
1 cup milk	2 large trout or flounder, dressed

- Sauté onion, celery, shallots, and garlic in margarine until soft; blend in flour. Add milk and white wine; cook until thickened.

- Add shrimp, crab, and parsley; mix in bread crumbs.

- Open fish along backbone and fill with stuffing. Place in a greased baking dish and cover tightly.

- Bake at 350° for 45 minutes; uncover and bake an additional 15 minutes.

Yield: 2 large stuffed fish

Jean Hiott

SALMON CROQUETTES

1 (8-ounce) can sockeye salmon	7-10 saltines, crushed
½ teaspoon dill	black pepper to taste
½ teaspoon parsley	2 teaspoons grated onion
1 egg	(optional)
¼ teaspoon lemon juice	2 tablespoons butter, melted

- Remove skin and bone from salmon.

- Combine salmon and remaining ingredients; mix well.

- Shape into patties and brown in butter in a skillet.

Yield: 2 or 3 servings

Anne and Tom Peterson

FLOUNDER FANTASY

8 filets of flounder
3 tablespoons lemon juice
salt and pepper to taste
¾ pound shrimp, cooked, peeled,
  and sliced in half lengthwise
½ pound mushrooms, thinly sliced

½ pound shallots, finely chopped
2 cans cream of celery soup,
  undiluted
2 tablespoons green Chartreuse
¼ cup Parmesan cheese

- Arrange filets in a greased baking dish; sprinkle with lemon juice, salt, and pepper.

- Arrange shrimp, mushrooms, and shallots over filets; cover with soup that has been mixed with Chartreuse.

- Bake at 350° for 15 to 20 minutes; remove from oven and sprinkle with cheese.

- Set oven to broil; place fish under broiler until lightly browned.

Yield: 8 servings

TOMATO-MUSTARD SAUCE

Wonderful with grilled dolphin!

2 tomatoes, peeled and diced
1 cup prepared mustard
2 tablespoons mayonnaise
2 tablespoons Chardonnay
½ cup olive oil
1 tablespoon lemon juice
1 tablespoon orange juice
2 cloves garlic

1 Vidalia onion, quartered
dash of Worcestershire sauce
dash of Tabasco
1 teaspoon dill
1 teaspoon oregano
½ teaspoon cracked black pepper
½ cup fresh basil

- Place all ingredients in food processor and blend. Refrigerate until ready to use.

Yield: 3 cups

116

BAKED WHOLE SEA BASS

1 (5-pound) sea bass, cleaned and
dried, head and tail attached
salt and pepper to taste
½ cup butter, melted

¼ cup sliced blanched almonds
3 slices bacon
¼ cup chopped parsley for garnish
lemon slices for garnish

- Sprinkle bass with salt and pepper, inside and out. Lay fish in a greased baking dish.

- Sauté almonds in butter over low heat. Brush fish with ¼ of melted butter; lay bacon on top.

- Bake at 350° for 45 minutes, basting every 10 minutes with butter-almond mixture.

- Place foil over fish so almonds do not burn. Increase temperature to 375° for 15 minutes more. Remove from oven; test for doneness. (Fish will flake easily with a fork when done.)

Yield: 8 to 10 servings

If you leave the head and tail on big fish when baking, the meat will be moist.

Aimee Kornegay

TARTAR SAUCE

¼ teaspoon Tabasco
1 tablespoon lemon juice
1 cup mayonnaise
1 tablespoon minced onion
1 tablespoon chopped parsley

2 tablespoons chopped
stuffed olives
2 tablespoons chopped
sweet pickles

- Stir Tabasco and lemon juice into mayonnaise. Add remaining ingredients; mix well. Chill until ready to serve.

Yield: 1¼ cups

Aimee Kornegay

RASPBERRY SALMON

4 salmon filets, washed and dried
freshly ground black pepper
olive oil
1 sweet onion, sliced

6 tablespoons raspberry preserves
3 tablespoons water
lemon slices for garnish

- Season filets with pepper and set aside.

- Rub sauté pan with oil and heat until hot. Sear salmon on both sides and allow to cook just until almost done. Remove salmon from pan to a platter.

- Sauté onion rings until transparent; place on platter with salmon.

- Put preserves and water in sauté pan and mix until blended and warm.

- Return salmon and onions to pan with raspberry sauce to finish cooking.

- Serve topped with onion rings, sauce, and lemon slices.

  Yield: 4 servings

Mary Dean Richards

LEMON BUTTER SAUCE

½ cup butter
2 tablespoons lemon juice
2 tablespoons minced parsley

1 tablespoon finely chopped
lemon zest

- Melt butter in a saucepan over low heat; stir in remaining ingredients.

  Yield: ½ cup

Aimee Nelson

"And Jesus said to them,
'Follow me and I will make you
fishers of men'."
Matthew 4:19

GAME

GAME

Edisto Island Mustard Fried Marsh Hens
Dove Breasts
Potted Doves with Brown Gravy
Doves Camden Style
Dove Breast Stroganoff
Baked Quail
Texas Quail
Smothered Quail
Roasted Rare Duck
Belser Roasted Wild Duck
Roast Wild Duck with Mushroom Gravy
Duck Lachicotte
Wild Ducks or Geese
Goose Liver Pâté
Edisto Wild Turkey & Venison Pilau
Roasted Wild Turkey
Venison Steak with Green Peppercorn Sauce
Venison Roast
Venison Roast a la Rowe
∝ Venison Roast a la Becky
∝ German Sweet Sauce for Venison
Venison Meat Loaf
Mustard Fried Venison Cube Steak
Venison Vegetable Soup
Demi's Venison Jerky

"…Isaac said, 'Now then,
please take your gear,
your quiver and your bow,
and go out to the field
and hunt game for me'."
Genesis 27:2, 3

EDISTO ISLAND
MUSTARD FRIED MARSH HENS

marsh hens
3 tablespoons salt to 1 gallon water
garlic salt
seasoned salt
coarse ground black pepper

instant mashed potato flakes
self-rising flour
prepared mustard
burgundy wine
vegetable oil for frying

- Start with 1 box #8 shot, .410 gauge, 1 small boy, 1 old man, 1 jon boat, 1 push-pole, and one October 7-foot tide. Wash thoroughly after return trip home. Soak birds overnight in salted water. Store in refrigerator.

- Drain the birds the next day. Pat dry. Sprinkle liberally with garlic salt, seasoned salt, and coarse ground black pepper.

- Mix equal amounts of instant mashed potato flakes and self-rising flour. Set aside.

- Mix 2 parts prepared mustard and 1 part burgundy wine. Dip birds in wine-mustard mixture, shake in dry mixture.

- Fry until golden brown.

Yield: 2 birds per person

Parker Tuten

DOVE BREASTS

12 dove breasts with skin   garlic powder to taste
½ cup butter, melted   6 bacon strips, quartered
seasoned salt to taste

- Baste breasts with melted butter. Season lightly with seasoned salt and garlic powder.

- Place breasts close together in a 2-quart baking dish. Place 2 quartered strips of bacon across each breast.

- Bake at 350° for 20 minutes. If bacon is not crisp, place under broiler until brown.

Yield: 4 servings

Judy Inman

POTTED DOVES WITH BROWN GRAVY

12 whole doves, dressed   2½ to 3 cups water
seasoned salt   1 (4.5 ounce) can sliced mushrooms
garlic powder   Kitchen Bouquet®
self-rising flour   salt and pepper to taste
vegetable oil for frying   1 cup rice, cooked

- Season doves lightly with seasoned salt and garlic powder. Dredge in flour.

- Brown doves in hot vegetable oil. Remove birds from pan and drain. Pour off excess oil and leave pan drippings. Add 6 to 8 tablespoons of flour to drippings, stirring constantly until golden brown and thick.

- Pour in water and stir until gravy is of desired consistency. Add mushrooms, Kitchen Bouquet, salt, and pepper.

- Serve gravy over doves and rice.

Yield: 4 servings

Judy Inman

DOVES CAMDEN STYLE

16 doves, dressed
salt and pepper to taste
8 slices bacon
⅛ teaspoon Tabasco
4 tablespoons Worcestershire
   sauce

⅔ cup liquid: water, wine,
   or consommé
12 ounces mushrooms, sliced
2 tablespoons butter
1 teaspoon lemon juice
chopped parsley for garnish

- Pat doves dry. Salt and pepper doves inside and out; dust lightly with flour.

- Cook bacon until crisp in a large Dutch oven. Remove bacon. Brown doves on all sides in bacon drippings.

- Arrange doves breast side down in a single layer. Turn fire low. Add Tabasco, Worcestershire, and liquid. Cover and cook 20 minutes.

- Stir and turn doves breast up. Cook covered for 20 minutes. Add more liquid if necessary.

- Sauté mushrooms lightly in butter and lemon juice while doves are cooking. Add mushrooms to doves for last 15 minutes of cooking.

- Crumble bacon over doves and garnish with parsley.

Yield: 8 servings

8 teal may be substituted for doves.

Aimee Kornegay

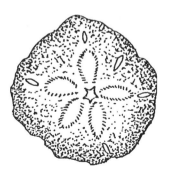

DOVE BREAST STROGANOFF

12 whole doves or breasts, dressed
salt and pepper to taste
2 tablespoons butter, melted
1 medium onion, chopped
1 can cream of celery soup,
  undiluted

1 (4-ounce) can mushrooms
½ cup Sauterne
½ teaspoon rosemary
½ teaspoon oregano
1 teaspoon Kitchen Bouquet
1 cup sour cream

- Arrange doves in baking dish. Salt and pepper lightly.

- Sauté onion in butter until soft. Stir in soup and next 5 ingredients. Pour sauce over doves. Cover dish lightly with foil.

- Bake at 325° for I hour, turning doves from time to time.

- Remove doves from baking dish. Stir sour cream into sauce. Return doves to dish and bake for 30 minutes.

Yield: 4 to 6 servings

Serve doves and sauce over wild rice; quail may be substituted.

Timmy Dorn

BAKED QUAIL

12 quail, dressed
½ cup butter
1 onion, chopped
1 pound fresh mushrooms, chopped

1 can cream of celery soup
1 can cream of mushroom soup
⅓ cup dry sherry

- Brown quail in butter and place in a baking dish.

- Sauté onion and mushrooms in butter.

- Add onion and mushrooms, butter, and remaining ingredients to quail and cover with foil.

- Bake at 375° for 30 minutes.

Yield: 12 servings

Serve with yellow rice; makes lots of gravy.

Ann Parler

TEXAS QUAIL

½ cup butter, melted
12 to 16 quail, dressed
1 cup chicken broth
1 cup vermouth

½ teaspoon salt
¼ teaspoon black pepper
2 cups whipping cream

- Melt butter in a large baking dish. Roll quail in butter, coating completely; cover with foil.

- Bake at 300° for 2 hours; turn once.

- Drain liquid into a sauce pan and add broth, vermouth, salt, and pepper; boil until reduced, may thicken with cornstarch.

- Add cream; boil 2 minutes and pour over quail.

- Bake at 325° for 1 hour.

  Yield: 6 to 8 servings

Ann Parler

SMOTHERED QUAIL

8 quail, dressed
½ cup butter
4 tablespoons flour

2 cups chicken broth
½ cup dry sherry
salt and pepper to taste

- Brown quail in butter in a heavy skillet; remove to a deep baking dish.

- Add flour to butter in skillet and stir well. Slowly add chicken broth and sherry; blend well and add salt and pepper.

- Bring to a boil; pour sauce over quail; cover tightly.

- Bake at 350° for 1 hour.

  Yield: 8 servings

V. V. Thompson

ROASTED RARE DUCK

*Most people who eat duck prepared in this manner
think that this is the best way to cook ducks.*

4 medium ducks, dressed   black pepper to taste
garlic salt to taste   2 onions, quartered

- Season ducks inside and outside with garlic salt and pepper. Place onions in duck cavities.

- Preheat gas or charcoal grill until hot. Cook ducks 15 to 25 minutes, turning often so not to burn.

Yield: 1 duck per person

Tom Kapp

Fill duck cavity with celery. Rub outside of duck heavily with salt. Bake at 500° for 20 minutes.

Buddy Rowe

BELSER ROASTED WILD DUCK

1 pound link sausage   salt and pepper to taste
2 large onions, sliced   pinch of sage
1 cup rice   1 can consommé
2 medium ducks   4 slices bacon

- Fry sausage and cut links in half. Remove from pan. Sauté onion in grease until tender. Place rice in onion mixture and stir until each grain is coated with grease.

- Place rice, onion, and sausage in a roaster and pour consommé over all.

- Season ducks with salt, pepper, and sage. Place ducks on top of rice and cover ducks with bacon.

- Bake, covered, at 250° for 5 hours.

Yield: 2 to 4 servings

Ritchie Belser

ROAST WILD DUCK
WITH MUSHROOM GRAVY

4 ducks, dressed and giblets chopped	pinch of oregano to taste (optional)
1 quart vinegar	pinch of basil to taste (optional)
1 quart water	2 onions halved
½ cup butter, melted	2 apples halved
poultry seasoning to taste	2 celery hearts halved
paprika to taste	4 bay leaves
seasoned salt to taste	orange slices (optional)
garlic powder to taste	½ cup dry red wine
pinch of thyme to taste (optional)	½ cup orange marmalade

- Combine vinegar and water in large container and soak ducks overnight. Rinse off ducks and pat dry.

- Baste ducks with butter. Season lightly with poultry seasoning and paprika. Season heavily with seasoned salt. Season lightly with garlic powder. Stuff each duck with onion, apple, celery, and a bay leaf. Place orange slice on breasts if desired. Place ducks and giblets in a roaster pan with tight lid or cover roaster tightly with foil.

- Bake at 450° for 30 minutes. Reduce oven to 325° and bake for an additional 2 hours.

- Uncover ducks, add wine and glaze ducks with marmalade. Bake at 400° for an additional 30 minutes.

- Prepare gravy. Serve with ducks.

GRAVY

1 (4.5 ounce) can chopped mushrooms	salt and pepper to taste

- Pour liquid from roaster into a medium saucepan. Remove only onions from duck cavity, chop, and place in saucepan with liquid. Add mushrooms and pre-cooked giblets. Add enough water and flour for gravy. Mix well. Season with salt and pepper.

Yield: 4 to 6 servings

Fred Inman

DUCK LACHICOTTE

Different, delicious, and always a hit!

1 (16-ounce) can whole cranberry sauce	2 ounces soy sauce
	2 ounces Worcestershire sauce
1 package dry onion soup mix	4 tablespoons (heaping) flour
1 (8-ounce) bottle Russian salad dressing	4 medium ducks, dressed

- Combine cranberry sauce, onion soup mix, and Russian dressing. Set aside.

- Mix soy sauce, Worcestershire, and flour. Stir into cranberry mixture. Pour small amount of sauce into each duck cavity and roll duck over and over to coat inside of each duck with sauce. Fill duck cavities with apple, celery, and onion.

- Place ducks into a baking dish prepared with cooking spray and pour remaining sauce over ducks. Cover dish tightly with foil.

- Bake at 400° for 2½ hours. Remove from oven and let ducks cool down for about 30 minutes. Do not remove foil during this time.

Yield: 4 servings

Serve with rice and pour remaining sauce over rice and ducks.

Chip Lachicotte

Substitute turkey, chicken, pork, or venison for duck.

WILD DUCKS OR GEESE

Simple to cook and wonderful!

For each duck:
½ small onion
1 stalk celery, cut in 1 inch pieces

½ bell pepper, cut in large pieces
3 bacon slices
1 tablespoon olive oil

- Place onion, celery, pepper, and 1 bacon slice inside each duck cavity.

- Line baking dish with aluminum foil. Place ducks in dish. Place 2 bacon slices over the breast and brush olive oil over each duck.

- Prepare sauce. Pour sauce over the ducks and allow extra sauce to run over into baking dish. Cover and seal baking dish very tightly with foil.

- Bake at 325° for at least 2 hours or until tender.

SAUCE

For each duck:
2½ ounces tomato ketchup
1½ ounces Worcestershire sauce
1 teaspoon hot pepper sauce

½ teaspoon Tabasco
2½ ounces dry sherry
1 teaspoon olive oil
1 clove of garlic, minced

- Mix all ingredients thoroughly.

Yield: 1 duck per person

Good served with wild rice and a hot fruit casserole.

Van Leer Rowe

Follow same directions for cooking a wild goose, only triple sauce recipe. Bake at 325° for 2½ to 3 hours or until tender.

GOOSE LIVER PÂTÉ

This is a spread and great for parties.

½ cup butter, melted
1 small onion, chopped
1 clove garlic, minced
1 cup goose liver

¼ cup clarified butter
salt and pepper to taste
pinch of thyme
1 tablespoon brandy

- Sauté onions and garlic in butter until soft. Add livers and increase heat to medium. Sauté briskly until livers are firm.

- Cool livers. Purée in blender until smooth. Add clarified butter and beat into mixture. Season with salt, pepper, and thyme. Mix in brandy.

- Chill. Spread on crackers or melba rounds.

Yield: 1 cup

Van Leer Rowe

May substitute chicken livers for goose livers.

EDISTO WILD TURKEY & VENISON PILAU

2 turkey legs and thighs
½ cup diced onion
½ cup diced bell pepper
1 pound bulk venison sausage

¼ cup margarine
1 can cream of mushroom soup
1 cup rice

- Simmer turkey legs and thighs in enough water to cover until very tender, about 6 hours. Drain, reserving 3 cups broth. Cut or tear turkey into bite-size pieces and set aside.

- Sauté onion, peppers, and sausage, stirring to crumble, in margarine until sausage is done, about 25 minutes.

- Combine broth with soup in a large saucepan; add turkey and sausage mixture; bring to a boil, reduce heat, and simmer for 20 minutes. Add rice and cook about 25 to 30 minutes or until rice is done.

Yield: 10 to 12 servings

Buddy Rowe

Game

ROASTED WILD TURKEY

1 8 pound wild turkey	pinch of thyme, tarragon, and sage
1 cup butter, divided	coarse black pepper to taste
liver of turkey	bacon slices
1 mild onion, quartered	2 cups chicken broth
2 celery hearts, cut in thirds	

- Rub turkey inside and out with ½ cup of butter. Place liver and next 6 ingredients in turkey cavity. Cover breast and all exposed parts with bacon slices.

- Bake at 400° for 1 hour.

- Remove turkey from oven and reduce heat to 350°. Remove bacon from turkey.

- Warm chicken broth and remaining butter in a sauce pan. Return turkey to oven and bake for another hour, basting with broth from saucepan every 5 to 10 minutes. Check turkey for doneness. Leg should move easily.

- Transfer turkey to an ovenproof platter and return to oven. Turn off heat and leave bird in oven for 10 to 15 minutes.

Yield: 8 servings

Ritchie Belser

131

VENISON STEAK
WITH GREEN PEPPERCORN SAUCE

Easy to prepare!

4 (8-ounce) venison steaks,   2 tablespoons olive oil
   cut 1 inch thick   salt and pepper to taste
2 to 3 cloves of garlic, minced

- Wash steaks and pat dry. Trim all visible fat.

- Combine garlic and olive oil. Pour marinade over steaks. Marinate in refrigerator for 2 to 4 hours.

- Season with salt and pepper. Broil or grill to desired degree of doneness.

- Prepare Green Peppercorn Sauce. Pour sauce over steaks and serve immediately.

GREEN PEPPERCORN SAUCE

4 tablespoons unsalted butter   salt and pepper to taste
¼ cup whole green peppercorns   1 tablespoon cognac

- Melt butter in saucepan. Stir in remaining ingredients.

- Bring to a boil, stirring constantly, until thoroughly heated.

Yield: 4 servings

David Gallup

Come Heavenly Father, Our Guest to be,
And bless these gifts bestowed by Thee.
Bless our loved ones everywhere,
And keep them in Thy tender care.
Amen.

VENISON ROAST

This recipe is from my sister-in-law, Sarah Eggleston.
She is a great meat cook, especially venison.

1 Venison roast, frozen	1 medium onion, chopped
seasoned meat tenderizer	1 small jar guava jelly or
bacon slices	red wine jelly (optional)

- Rub frozen venison heavily with seasoned meat tenderizer. Let thaw completely.

- Cut several slices in roast and stuff with onion and pieces of bacon. Place several slices of bacon on top of roast. Spread jelly on top of roast.

- Bake at 300° for 20 minutes per pound. Do not overcook.

Yield: 4 to 6 servings

Gale Belser

VENISON ROAST A LA ROWE

This is easy to prepare and one of my husband's favorites!

1 venison roast, dressed	1 tablespoon honey
bacon, cut in pieces	1 tablespoon prepared mustard
1 package dry onion soup mix	½ cup dry red wine
1 can cream of mushroom soup,	3 tablespoon olive oil
undiluted	juice of ½ lime
3 cloves garlic, minced	

- Place roast in casserole dish and make several slices into meat. Insert bacon pieces.

- Combine in a small bowl onion soup mix and next 7 ingredients. Pour over meat. Cover meat with 4 or 5 strips of bacon. Cover casserole tightly with foil.

- Bake at 325° for 2 to 3 hours depending on size of roast. Do not overcook.

Yield: 6 to 8 servings

Van Leer Rowe

May substitute a venison ham or beef roast for venison roast.

133

VENISON ROAST A LA BECKY

3 to 4 pound venison roast
1 cup mushrooms
1 can beef bouillon
1½ cups water
1 cup Burgundy wine

½ teaspoon garlic powder
  (or 2 cloves garlic, minced)
⅔ cups finely chopped onion
½ teaspoon basil

- Place meat and mushrooms in a large bowl. Pierce meat with a large fork in many places.

- Mix bouillon and next 5 ingredients; pour mixture over meat. Be sure the meat is covered with liquid.

- Cover bowl and refrigerate for 3 days.

- Prepare seasoning mixture.

- Remove meat from marinade (reserve) and blot dry.

- Coat the meat with seasoning mixture and rub in as much as possible.

- Brown meat in oil in a large flat baking pan which has a cover.

- Pour marinade over meat.

- Bake, covered, at 350° for 3 hours or until tender.

SEASONING MIXTURE

½ cup flour
1½ teaspoons salt
¼ teaspoon black pepper

¼ teaspoon thyme
¼ teaspoon basil
½ teaspoon paprika

- Mix flour and remaining ingredients.

  Yield: 6 servings

Rebecca Whaley

GERMAN SWEET SAUCE ⌒✕ FOR VENISON

This was taken from a very old French cookbook.

1 can pie cherries	½ peel of lemon
1 stick cinnamon	¼ cup red wine
6 cloves	¼ cup sugar

- Stew cherries, cinnamon, cloves, and lemon peel until very soft, about 20 minutes.

- Run through a sieve; add red wine and sugar.

- Taste and if not sweet enough, add a little more sugar.

Yield: about 2 cups

Rebecca Whaley

VENISON MEAT LOAF

2 eggs, beaten	⅛ teaspoon black pepper
1 (8-ounce) can tomato sauce	1½ pounds ground venison
1 medium onion, finely chopped	2 tablespoons brown sugar
1 cup dry bread crumbs	2 tablespoons spicy brown mustard
1½ teaspoons salt	2 tablespoons vinegar

- Combine in a large bowl eggs and next 5 ingredients. Add venison and mix well. Press into an ungreased 9x5x3-inch loaf pan.

- Mix brown sugar, mustard, and vinegar. Pour over meat mixture.

- Bake at 350° for 1 hour and 10 minutes.

Yield: 6 to 8 servings

Missy Camp

MUSTARD FRIED VENISON CUBE STEAK

This is so easy to prepare and is one of the best ways to serve venison.

1 pound venison cubed steak
salt and pepper to taste
garlic powder to taste
½ cup Dijon mustard

1 tablespoon olive oil
flour for dredging
vegetable oil

- Cut steaks into 2x1-inch strips. Season meat with salt, pepper, and garlic powder.

- Combine mustard and olive oil. Brush both sides of meat with mustard mixture. Dredge in flour.

- Sauté venison in oil turning and cooking until lightly browned on both sides.

Yield: 4 servings

May use venison tenderloin cut in ¼ inch medallions.

Van Leer Rowe

In brown bag, pour flour, salt, and pepper to taste, then add more. Cover venison pieces with prepared yellow mustard. Throw in bag and shake, then put in hot deep grease. When venison floats, it's ready! Serve with grits, if you can get it to the table!

Jenks Mikell

VENISON VEGETABLE SOUP

Serve with hot French garlic bread,
and you have a complete meal on a cold winter night.

1 pound ground venison
1 (8-ounce) can tomato sauce
1 (14½-ounce) can diced tomatoes
1 (46-ounce) can vegetable juice

1 (16-ounce) package frozen
   sliced okra
1 (16-ounce) package frozen
   mixed vegetables
salt and pepper to taste

- Brown meat. Add tomato sauce, diced tomatoes, and vegetable juice. Bring to a boil, reduce heat, cover, and simmer 15 minutes.

- Add frozen vegetables and season with salt and pepper.

- Bring to a boil, reduce heat, and simmer about 1 hour 30 minutes, stirring occasionally.

Yield: 6 to 8 servings

Van Leer Rowe

"As the deer pants for the water brooks,
so my soul pants for Thee, O God."
Psalm 42:1

DEMI'S VENISON JERKY

1 medium venison ham, well trimmed	3 tablespoons smoky flavored sauce
1 cup soy sauce	1 tablespoon garlic powder
¾ cup Worcestershire sauce	½ teaspoon black pepper
½ cup red wine vinegar	½ teaspoon Tabasco

- Separate meat from bone by "rolling" at natural divisions and cutting from bone. Cut meat long way into ¼-inch to ⅜-inch strips. Trim off fat and sinew as much as possible.

- Mix soy sauce and remaining ingredients and marinate strips 12 to 24 hours, or until meat has absorbed marinade sauce well.

- Place aluminum foil on bottom of oven to catch drippings.

- Drain marinade (do not reuse) and hang strips of meat from top rack of oven using toothpicks.

- Bake at 125° to 150° for 12 to 16 hours, or until dry but not brittle.

Back straps or other tender cuts work well as jerky. In place of smoky flavored sauce, meat can be dried in a smoker. Follow cooker instructions. Adjust marinade amount and/or time if less meat is used. Meat should not be packed tightly in marinade container.

Demi Howard

POULTRY

POULTRY

Coronation Chicken
"The Man's" Hot Chicken Salad
Hot Chicken Salad
Muma's BBQ Chicken
Lemon Chicken Garlic
Chicken Parmesan
Petey's Chicken Supreme
Hawaiian Chicken
Honey-Lime & Mustard Chicken
Easy Street Chicken
St. George Chicken
Chicken with Broccoli
Chicken & Wild Rice
Texas Chicken
Poppy Seed Chicken
Curried Chicken Casserole
Deluxe Chicken Casserole
Turkey with Maple Syrup
Turkey Crunch for a Bunch
Gourmet Turkey Enchilada Casserole
Chicken Breasts with Crabmeat Stuffing

"I know every bird of the mountains,
and everything that moves in the field is Mine."
Psalm 50:11

CORONATION CHICKEN

"A court favorite" from St. James the Great Church of England.

1 cooked chicken, cut into
  bite-size pieces
seedless grapes, halved
5 tablespoons mayonnaise

1 tablespoon mango chutney
½ teaspoon curry powder
1 teaspoon dried tarragon

- Mix all ingredients and serve.

Yield: 6 servings

Mercia Hayes
Frances Richardson

"THE MAN'S" HOT CHICKEN SALAD

8 chicken breasts, cooked
  and boned
1 bottle clear French dressing
1 cup chopped celery
1 cup mayonnaise

1 cup chopped pecans or almonds
  (optional)
1 pound jar pasteurized processed
  cheese spread
1 can French fried onion rings

- Cut chicken into bite-size pieces; toss in French dressing and marinate overnight.

- Add celery, mayonnaise, and nuts; mix well. Place in a 13x9x2-inch baking dish and cover with cheese spread.

- Bake at 350° for 30 minutes; top with onions and bake 5 minutes longer.

Yield: 8 servings

Brian A. Nelson

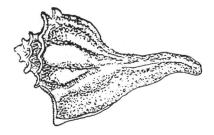

HOT CHICKEN SALAD

Great to serve at a luncheon.

3 cups cooked chicken
2 cups sliced celery
½ cup slivered almonds
½ cup sliced water chestnuts
¼ cup chopped pimento
1 cup mayonnaise
½ cup sour cream

3 tablespoons lemon juice
2 tablespoons grated onion
½ teaspoon salt
¼ teaspoon black pepper
1 cup Chinese noodles
½ cup grated cheddar cheese

- Mix chicken and next 4 ingredients together.

- Blend mayonnaise with next 5 ingredients. Mix mayonnaise mixture with chicken mixture.

- Pour into a greased 2-quart casserole. Put noodles and cheese on top.

- Bake at 350° for 30 minutes.

  Yield: 6 to 8 servings

Beth Barker

Substitute ½ can cream of mushroom soup for sour cream, 1 cup crushed potato chips for Chinese noodles, and add ½ teaspoon prepared mustard.

Mary Crawford

MUMA'S BBQ CHICKEN

Anyone who likes vinegar will love this chicken!

1 fryer, cut-up	2 slices bacon
salt and pepper to taste	1½ cups water

- Place chicken in a 13x9x2-inch baking dish. Sprinkle with salt and lots of pepper. Place 2 slices of bacon on chicken. Pour water around chicken.

- Bake at 400° for 1 hour or until brown and done. Remove from oven.

- Prepare sauce. Pour sauce over chicken and return to oven until gravy thickens and is golden in color.

BBQ Sauce

½ cup flour	1 cup apple cider vinegar

- Mix flour in enough water to make a paste. Gradually add warm water to this to make 1½ cups. Blend in vinegar.

Yield: 4 servings

This is my Grandmother's recipe and a family favorite for years.

Martha Whetstone

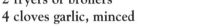

LEMON CHICKEN GARLIC

2 fryers or broilers	juice of 4 lemons
4 cloves garlic, minced	coarse salt

- Salt chickens inside and outside. Pour lemon juice and minced garlic over chicken.

- Bake at 400° for 1 hour, basting occasionally.

- Turn off oven and let chicken sit for awhile. Juice will caramelize.

Yield: 6 to 8 servings

Kitsy Westmoreland

CHICKEN PARMESAN

8 whole chicken breasts, halved
  and boned
½ cup butter, melted
1 cup Parmesan cheese

¾ cup seasoned bread crumbs
½ teaspoon oregano
½ teaspoon black pepper
½ teaspoon garlic powder

- Mix cheese, crumbs, and seasonings. Dip chicken in butter, then coat in crumb mixture.

- Arrange chicken in a 13x9x2-inch baking dish, skin side up.

- Bake at 350° for 55 minutes. Serve with rice pilaf.

Yield: 16 servings

For a slightly different flavor, add 1 teaspoon sherry to each piece of chicken last 10 minutes of cooking.

PETEY'S CHICKEN SUPREME

2 (3-ounce) jars dried chipped beef
8 boneless, skinless chicken
  breasts

8 slices bacon
2 cups sour cream
2 cans cream of mushroom soup

- Spread beef over bottom of a greased 13x9x2-inch glass casserole dish. Wrap chicken breasts with bacon and lay on top of chipped beef. Mix cream and soup and pour over all. Cover with foil.

- Bake at 300° for 2 hours. Remove foil and bake 1 hour until nicely browned.

Yield: 8 servings

Aimee Nelson

HAWAIIAN CHICKEN

Easy and may be prepared ahead.

8 to 12 chicken pieces with skin
1 can cream of mushroom soup
1 (8-ounce) bottle French
  dressing
1 (16-ounce) can whole berry
  cranberry sauce
1 package dry onion soup mix

- Place chicken pieces in a greased 13x9x2-inch casserole dish.
- Mix soup, dressing, cranberries, and soup mix. Pour mixture over chicken.
- Bake, covered, at 350° for 1 hour. Uncover and bake for 30 minutes.

Yield: 8 to 12 servings

Susalee Sasser

HONEY-LIME & MUSTARD CHICKEN

6 boneless, skinless chicken
  breasts
3 tablespoons honey
1½ tablespoons coarse mustard
2 tablespoons lime juice
salt to taste (optional)
2 packages long grain wild rice
1½ cups consommé
1 tablespoon butter, melted

- Pound chicken to ½-inch thickness; set aside.
- Combine honey, mustard, lime juice, and salt; mix well and pour over chicken. Marinate at room temperature for 15 minutes turning once.
- Cook rice in a steamer with consommé and flavor packets for 30 minutes.
- Remove chicken from marinade; reserve marinade.
- Combine chicken and butter in a 12-inch skillet and cook 4 to 5 minutes per side or until chicken is done. Remove to a serving platter; keep warm. Add reserved marinade to skillet and reduce over high heat for 2 minutes. Spoon over chicken; serve with rice.

Yield 6 servings

Brian A. Nelson

145

EASY STREET CHICKEN

4 chicken breasts, boned and
  skin removed
1 package dried beef
1 cup sharp cheddar cheese,
  grated and divided

black pepper to taste
1 can cream of mushroom soup
½ cup white wine

- Place chicken breasts on pieces of dried beef. Sprinkle with ¾ cup cheese and season with pepper. Wrap the dried beef around the breasts. Lay seam side down in a small greased casserole dish.

- Mix soup with wine and pour over chicken. Sprinkle with remaining cheese.

- Bake at 300° for 2 hours or until tender.

Yield: 4 servings

Les Blankin

ST. GEORGE CHICKEN

2 fryers, cooked and boned
1 small can pimentos, chopped
  and drained
1 can sliced water chestnuts,
  drained
2 cups cooked rice
2 cans cream of chicken soup

1½ cups mayonnaise
2 cups chopped celery
2 medium onions, chopped fine
2 cups round buttery cheese
  crackers, crumbled
¼ cup butter, melted

- Chop chicken into large pieces; combine chicken with next 8 ingredients, reserving ½ the cracker crumbs.

- Spoon mixture into a 13x9x2-inch casserole dish; top with remaining crumbs and drizzle with melted butter.

- Bake at 350° for 35 to 45 minutes.

Yield: 6 to 8 servings

Barbara Hood

CHICKEN WITH BROCCOLI

3 whole boned chicken breasts
2 packages frozen broccoli spears
2 cans cream of chicken soup
1 cup mayonnaise
1 teaspoon lemon juice

1 tablespoon butter, melted
½ teaspoon curry powder
½ cup grated sharp cheese
½ cup bread or cracker crumbs

- Arrange chicken and broccoli in a 13x9x2-inch glass dish.

- Mix soup with next 4 ingredients and spread over chicken and broccoli. Mix cheese with crumbs and spread on top of mixture.

- Bake at 350° for 45 minutes.

Joan Foxworth

CHICKEN & WILD RICE

5 to 6 pounds chicken breasts
  cooked and boned
3 (6½-ounce) boxes
  quick-cooking wild rice
1 large onion, chopped
½ cup butter or margarine
6 tablespoons flour

2½ cups milk
3 cans mushroom soup
2 (3-ounce) cans sliced
  mushrooms, drained
1½ teaspoon salt
½ teaspoon black pepper
1 pound cheddar cheese, grated

- Cut chicken into bite size pieces. Set aside.

- Cook rice according to box directions. Set aside.

- Sauté onion in butter until transparent. Add flour. Mix milk and soup; add to onion and flour. Add mushrooms, salt, and pepper. Set aside.

- Grease two 13x9x2-inch glass baking dishes. Layer sauce on bottom of each dish; next layer rice; then chicken; then remainder of sauce and cheese.

- Bake at 350° for 1 hour or until done.

Yield: 20 servings

Aimee Nelson

TEXAS CHICKEN

4 cups chopped, cooked chicken
2 cups bread, broken in pieces
2 cups cooked rice
1½ cups chicken broth
1½ cups milk
4 eggs, beaten
¼ cup chopped pimentos
¼ cup chopped bell pepper

1 (3-ounce) can sliced
   mushrooms, drained
½ cup slivered almonds, toasted
6 tablespoons butter
dash of salt
dash of black pepper
dash of paprika

- Combine chicken with remaining ingredients. Spoon into a large greased casserole.

- Bake at 350° for 1 hour. Let sit 10 minutes. Cut into squares.

- Prepare sauce and serve.

SAUCE

1 can mushroom soup
1 cup sour cream
4 tablespoons chopped pimentos

4 tablespoons milk
¼ cup white wine

- Combine soup, sour cream, pimentos, and milk. Heat stirring constantly. Do not let boil. Blend in wine.

Yield: 8 to 10 servings

This freezes well.

Barbara Hood

POPPY SEED CHICKEN

4 cups cooked chicken, cut in large pieces	1½ cups round buttery cracker crumbs
1 cup sour cream	¼ cup margarine
1 can cream of chicken soup	2 tablespoons poppy seeds
1 to 2 tablespoons sherry (optional)	

- Combine chicken, sour cream, and soup and place in a 13x9x2-inch baking dish.
- Sprinkle with cracker crumbs and dot with margarine and sprinkle poppy seeds on top.
- Bake at 350° for 30 minutes.

Yield: 8 servings

Freezes well; but leave crumbs, margarine, and poppy seeds off until ready to bake.

Mary Alice Beck
Veda Godwin

CURRIED CHICKEN CASSEROLE

This is wonderful for a dinner party.

3 chickens, cooked and boned	1 tablespoon curry powder
2 (8-ounce) bottles cole slaw dressing	1 (11-ounce) can mandarin orange slices
2 cups mayonnaise	1 package sliced or slivered almonds
1½ cups seedless green grapes	

- Mix cooked chicken pieces with dressing and mayonnaise; add grapes and curry.
- Layer with orange slices and top with almonds just before baking.
- Bake at 350° for 30 to 40 minutes until bubbly.
- Serve over long grain and wild rice.

Yield: 10 to 12 servings

Joan Foxworth

149

DELUXE CHICKEN CASSEROLE

1½ cups cooked, diced chicken	¼ teaspoon cayenne pepper
2 teaspoons finely chopped onion	½ teaspoon black pepper
1 cup chopped celery	1 tablespoon lemon juice
½ cup chopped walnuts or pecans	¾ cup mayonnaise
1½ cups cooked rice	¼ cup water
1 can cream of chicken soup	3 hard-boiled eggs, sliced
½ teaspoon salt	2 cups crushed potato chips

- Mix chicken and next 9 ingredients. Combine mayonnaise and water. Add to chicken mixture and gently fold in egg slices.
- Place in a greased casserole dish and top with potato chips.
- Bake at 400° for 15 minutes or until bubbly.

Yield: 8 servings

Selina Lyman

TURKEY WITH MAPLE SYRUP

Simple and good.

2 tablespoons margarine, melted	1 teaspoon Dijon mustard
3 tablespoons maple syrup	1 turkey breast

- Mix margarine, maple syrup, and mustard.
- Cook turkey breast following directions on package, basting with syrup mixture.

Yield: 6 servings

TURKEY CRUNCH FOR A BUNCH

6 cups diced cooked turkey
4 hard-boiled eggs, chopped
2 (4-ounce) cans sliced mushrooms
1½ cups chopped celery
1 cup slivered almonds, blanched

3 tablespoons chopped onion
2 cans cream of mushroom soup
1½ cups mayonnaise
chow mein noodles

- Mix together turkey and next 5 ingredients.

- Stir soup into mayonnaise and toss with turkey mixture. Turn into a large baking dish or two 2-quart dishes. Sprinkle with noodles.

- Bake at 350° for 40 minutes or until bubbling.

Yield: 12 servings

A special blessing for turkey crunch is that it may be assembled well ahead of time except for noodles, which should be added just before baking.

Bert Hatch

GOURMET TURKEY ENCHILADA CASSEROLE

2 pounds ground turkey
1 small onion, chopped
1 (10-ounce) can enchilada sauce
1 (4.5-ounce) can chopped
  green chilies
1 can cream of mushroom soup

1 can cream of chicken soup
1 package taco seasonings
1 package (10-count) 10-inch soft
  flour tortillas, quartered
2 cups grated cheddar cheese
1 cup grated mozzarella cheese

- Brown turkey in a large skillet; add onion, sauté, and drain. Add next 5 ingredients and simmer 15 minutes.

- Layer ⅓ of tortillas in a greased 13x9x2-inch baking dish. Spread ⅓ of meat mixture on tortillas and top with ⅓ of cheeses. Repeat twice, ending with cheeses.

- Bake at 350° for 30 minutes. Cool 5 to 10 minutes before serving.

Kenny Driggers

CHICKEN BREASTS
WITH CRABMEAT STUFFING

12 chicken breast halves, boned
and skin removed
½ cup finely chopped onion
½ cup finely chopped celery
¼ cup finely chopped bell pepper
1 cup butter or margarine, melted
and divided
½ pound lump crabmeat

2 cups seasoned stuffing mix
1 egg, beaten
¼ teaspoon black pepper
¼ teaspoon garlic salt
¼ teaspoon Creole seasoning
2 cups corn flakes, crumbled
1 envelope Béarnaise sauce
(optional)

- Place chicken halves on sheet of waxed paper. Flatten chicken to ¼ inch thickness with mallet.

- Sauté onion, celery, and bell pepper in ¼ cup butter in a large skillet. Remove from heat. Add crabmeat and next 5 ingredients and ¼ cup melted butter and mix well.

- Spread ¼ cup crabmeat mixture on each chicken breast. Roll up jelly-roll fashion, pressing edges to seal. Cover and refrigerate 30 minutes.

- Dip each chicken roll in remaining ½ cup butter and dredge in corn flake crumbs. Place seam side down in a greased 13x9x2-inch baking dish.

- Bake, covered, at 350° for 45 minutes. Uncover and bake an additional 10 minutes or until golden brown.

- Prepare Béarnaise sauce according to package directions. Pour over chicken rolls and serve.

Yield: 12 servings

MEATS

MEATS

Marinated Filet of Beef
Shepherd's Pie
Beef Stroganoff
Marinade for Steaks & Roasts
Lasagna
Marinade for Pork Tenderloin
Marzetti
Chinese Beef
Fireside Chili
Spicy Chili
Crockpot Beef Barbecue
Horseradish Sauce
Summer Sausage
∝ Pork Chops & Apples
Veal Marsala
∝ Roast Pork
Overnight Smithfield Ham
Sweet & Sour Ham
Crockpot Pork Barbecue
Ham & Spinach Casserole
Hot Mustard
Jack Bone's Sauce
Favorite Meat Loaf
Glazed Corned Beef

"When you have eaten and are satisfied,
you shall bless the Lord your God
for the good land which He has given you."
Deuteronomy 8:10

MARINATED FILET OF BEEF

1 cup lemon juice   1 beef filet, well trimmed
1 cup soy sauce

* Combine lemon juice and soy sauce; pour over beef. Cover and refrigerate 24 hours turning several times.

* Remove beef from marinade and place in a shallow baking pan.

* Bake at 425° for 10 minutes; reduce heat to 350° and bake 25 minutes for rare or 35 minutes for medium.

* Remove from oven and allow to stand 10 minutes before slicing or cool completely at room temperature and slice for serving cold.

Yield: 8 to 10 servings

Great for a cocktail party, too! Allow 4 to 5 people per pound.

V. V. Thompson

SHEPHERD'S PIE

Children love this!

4 medium potatoes, cooked
¼ cup butter, softened
1 cup sour cream
1 (3-ounce) package cream
   cheese, softened
1½ cup grated extra sharp
   cheddar cheese, divided

salt and pepper to taste
1 pound ground round, browned
   and drained
1 (15-ounce) can LeSueur peas,
   drained

* Whip hot potatoes with butter, sour cream, cream cheese, ½ cup cheddar cheese, salt, and pepper. Set aside.

* Layer in a 2-quart casserole dish beef, peas, potatoes, and remaining cheese.

* Bake at 350° for 30 minutes.

Yield: 4 to 6 servings

Aimee Moore

BEEF STROGANOFF

2 pounds sirloin steak, cut into
   thin strips
¼ cup plus 2 tablespoons butter
1 medium onion, chopped
2 cloves garlic, minced
½ pound fresh mushrooms, sliced
2 tablespoons flour

½ teaspoon salt
dash of black pepper
1 can beef bouillon
½ cup dry white wine
1 cup sour cream
1 teaspoon Worcestershire sauce

- Brown beef strips in butter in a heavy bottom skillet over high heat; remove beef and set aside. Sauté onion, garlic, and mushrooms in skillet until tender. Remove from heat.

- Stir in flour, salt, and pepper; stir until smooth. Gradually add bouillon. Bring to a boil stirring often and cook until smooth and slightly thickened. Add beef, reduce heat, and simmer 15 minutes or until beef is tender.

- Add wine, sour cream, and Worcestershire just before serving. Serve over egg noodles or rice.

Yield: 6 to 8 servings

Stroganoff may be prepared through cooking of beef, then re-heated, adding last 3 ingredients just before serving.

Cindy Kapp

MARINADE FOR STEAKS & ROASTS

½ cup soy sauce
2 tablespoons Worcestershire sauce
1 teaspoon grated ginger
1 clove garlic, chopped

1 teaspoon salt
1 teaspoon dry mustard
½ cup oil

- Mix all ingredients thoroughly.

- Marinate meat in sauce overnight or at least 6 hours.

Yield: 1 cup

Ritchie Belser

LASAGNA

1 pound ground beef	1 box 2-inch noodles
garlic powder to taste	1 cup cottage cheese, divided
1 large can whole tomatoes, chopped	12 ounces Swiss cheese, grated
1 small can tomato paste	and divided
½ teaspoon salt	12 ounces mozzarella cheese,
¾ teaspoon black pepper	grated and divided
½ teaspoon oregano	parmesan cheese

- Brown beef in a skillet; drain and sprinkle with garlic powder.
- Stir in tomatoes and next 5 ingredients; simmer 20 minutes.
- Cook noodles as directed.
- Place 3 noodles in a 13x9x2-inch baking dish; cover with half of beef, sprinkle with half of cottage cheese and half of remaining cheeses. Repeat layers.
- Bake at 350° for 20 minutes or until bubbly.

Yield: 8 to 10 servings

Venison and home grown tomatoes may be substituted.

Cindy Kapp

MARINADE FOR PORK TENDERLOIN

¼ cup lemon juice	1 tablespoon lemon zest
¼ cup olive oil	pinch of ginger (optional)
¼ cup soy sauce	

- Combine all ingredients and marinate meat for several hours.

Yield: ¾ cup

V. V. Thompson

157

MARZETTI

2 pounds ground beef
1 pound ground pork
1 large bell pepper, chopped
1 large onion, chopped
2 cups celery, chopped
2 or 3 cloves garlic, minced
½ cup butter

2 cans tomato soup
1 can mushrooms, drained
salt and pepper to taste
1 pound egg noodles, cooked
1 pound cheddar cheese, grated
  and divided

- Brown beef and pork with next 4 ingredients in butter; add soup, mushrooms, salt, and pepper and mix well.

- Pour mixture over cooked noodles in a 13x9x2-inch baking dish; mix in half of cheese and sprinkle remaining half on top.

- Bake at 325° for 1 hour.

Yield: 8 to 10 servings

Selina Lyman

CHINESE BEEF

1 pound round steak
3 tablespoons soy sauce
2 tablespoons dry sherry
4 teaspoons cornstarch
¼ teaspoon sugar
⅛ teaspoon ginger

¼ cup oil
1 medium onion, sliced
1 bell pepper, sliced
½ small package mushrooms
sliced water chestnuts (optional)

- Slice steak thinly in diagonal strips; marinate in a mixture of next 5 ingredients.

- Pour oil into a wok or large skillet and heat. Stir fry onion, pepper, mushrooms, and chestnuts until onion is transparent. Remove vegetables and set aside.

- Stir fry beef to desired degree of doneness; add vegetables and mix well.

- Serve over steamed rice.

Yield: 3 to 4 servings

Frances Leitner

FIRESIDE CHILI

My favorite recipe for Friday nights of winter weekends on Edisto.

1½ pounds ground beef
1 large onion, chopped
1 clove garlic, minced
2 (4½-ounce) can stewed
    tomatoes

1 (16-ounce) can kidney beans,
    drained
1 (8-ounce) can tomato sauce
1 to 2 tablespoons chili powder
½ teaspoon liquid smoke
grated cheddar cheese

- Cook beef, onion, and garlic in a 4-quart sauce pan; drain.

- Add tomatoes and next 4 ingredients and stir.

- Simmer, uncovered, 30 minutes.

- Top each serving with cheese.

Yield: 6 servings

Janet Roberts

SPICY CHILI

Perfect on a cold winter's night.

2 medium onions, chopped
1 medium bell pepper, chopped
2 pounds lean ground beef,
    browned and drained
3 tablespoons chili powder

1 small can tomato paste
1 (15-ounce) can tomato sauce
1 bottle hot ketchup
3 cans hot chili beans

- Cook onions and peppers in a large saucepan in a small amount of water until tender. Combine with beef and cook over medium heat for 20 minutes.

- Stir in chili powder; mix well. Add tomato paste and sauce; mix well and cook for 20 minutes over medium heat stirring often. Add ketchup and chili beans; mix well and heat thoroughly.

Yield: 8 to 10 servings

Barbara Hood

CROCKPOT BEEF BARBECUE

1 (2½-pound) boneless chuck
   roast, trimmed of fat
2 medium onions, chopped
¾ cup cola carbonated beverage
¼ cup Worcestershire sauce
1 tablespoon apple cider vinegar
2 cloves garlic, minced

1 teaspoon beef bouillon granules
½ teaspoon dry mustard
½ teaspoon chili powder
¼ teaspoon ground red pepper
½ cup ketchup
2 teaspoons butter or margarine
6 hamburger buns

- Place roast and onions in a 4-quart slow cooker.

- Combine cola and next 7 ingredients; reserve ½ cup and place in refrigerator. Pour remaining mixture into slow cooker.

- Cover and cook on high for six hours or until roast is very tender. Drain and chop roast. Keep warm.

- Combine reserved cola mixture, ketchup, and butter in a small saucepan; cook over medium heat, stirring constantly, just until thoroughly heated.

- Pour over chopped roast stirring gently.

- Spoon onto buns; serve with potato chips and pickle spears if desired.

Yield: 6 servings

Barbara Hamlen

HORSERADISH SAUCE

1½ cups sour cream
⅓ cup prepared horseradish

½ teaspoon sugar
dash of salt

- Combine all ingredients and mix well.

Yield: 2 cups

Best made the day before, allowing flavors to blend.

V. V. Thompson

SUMMER SAUSAGE

5 pounds lean ground beef
  or venison
5 teaspoons quick salt
2½ teaspoons garlic salt

2½ teaspoons hickory salt
2½ teaspoons mustard seed
¾ teaspoon minced garlic

- Combine all ingredients; mix well and refrigerate in a covered bowl for 24 hours.

- Re-mix ingredients and refrigerate another 24 hours.

- Form into rolls of desired length.

- Bake at 175° for 8 hours.

- Cool; wrap and freeze.

Yield: 10 (8-ounce) rolls

Shannon Winton

PORK CHOPS & APPLES

1 cup ketchup
3 tablespoons cider vinegar
6 tablespoons brown sugar
¼ cup Worcestershire sauce
6 pork chops, ¼ inch thick,
  trimmed of fat

salt and pepper to taste
1 (20-ounce) can apple slices,
  drained
2 cups sliced onions

- Make sauce of ketchup, vinegar, brown sugar, and Worcestershire sauce.

- Sprinkle each side of pork chops with salt and pepper.

- Layer half of apples, half of onions in a 13x9x2 inch baking dish; cover with half of sauce. Lay pork chops over sauce and repeat layers of apples and onions. Pour remaining sauce on top. Cover tightly with foil.

- Bake at 375° for 1 to 1½ hours, removing foil for last 30 minutes.

Yield: 4 to 6 servings

Evelyn Ford

VEAL MARSALA

Very quick and absolutely delicious.

1 pound veal scallops, sliced ¼-inch thick and pounded thin	1 cup sliced mushrooms
salt and freshly ground pepper	½ cup dry Marsala wine
flour for dredging	1 cup chicken broth
½ cup butter	¼ cup lemon juice
¼ cup olive oil	1 tablespoon sugar (optional)
1 tablespoon minced garlic	¼ cup chopped parsley
	lemon slices and parsley for garnish

- Season veal on both sides with salt and pepper; lightly dredge with flour.

- Melt butter with olive oil in a skillet over medium-high heat. Sauté veal quickly, without browning, 1 to 2 minutes on each side and transfer to a serving platter.

- Sauté garlic and mushrooms in same skillet and spoon over veal.

- Add Marsala and next 4 ingredients to skillet. Bring to a quick boil, reducing liquid slightly. Pour over veal, garnish, and serve.

Yield: 4 servings

Judie Nye

ROAST PORK ⊂×

1 (8- to 10-pound) pork roast	3 onions, sliced
1 cup brown sugar	1 tablespoon Tabasco sauce
1 tablespoon salt	1 cup tomato ketchup
1 tablespoon black pepper	1 cup water
1 quart canned tomatoes	

- Rub pork with sugar, salt, and pepper; place in a roaster. Add tomatoes and remaining ingredients.

- Bake, covered, at 350° for 3½ hours, basting every 30 minutes.

Yield: 8 to 10 servings

Mary Ella Hackett

OVERNIGHT SMITHFIELD HAM

1 Smithfield ham	1 cup brown sugar
1 cup molasses	1 cup vinegar

- Scrub ham and place in a roaster; cover with water and add molasses, sugar, and vinegar.

- Bake, covered, at 350° until water boils. This takes about 1 hour. Allow ham to boil for 1 hour.

- Turn the oven off. <u>Do not open oven door until the next morning.</u>

- Prepare glaze and spread on ham which has been scored and cloved. Brown.

GLAZE

1 cup brown sugar	¼ cup sherry
1 tablespoon prepared mustard	

- Combine ingredients.

  Yield: 1 baked ham

SWEET & SOUR HAM

1 (16-ounce) can sliced peaches	½ cup sugar
3 cups cubed cooked ham	¼ cup vinegar
2 bell peppers, sliced	3 tablespoons soy sauce
1 cup chicken broth, divided	4 tablespoons cornstarch

- Drain fruit; reserve syrup.

- Combine fruit syrup, ham, peppers, ¾ cup broth, and remaining ingredients in a saucepan; bring to a boil and simmer 10 minutes.

- Blend cornstarch and remaining ¼ cup broth and add to ham mixture. Cook, stirring, for 2 minutes; add fruit. Serve over steamed rice.

  Yield: 6 servings

Randolph Berretta

CROCKPOT PORK BARBECUE

1 (5- or 6-pound) Boston butt
  pork roast
10 ounces tomato or mustard
  bottled barbecue sauce
1 tablespoon salt

1 teaspoon black pepper
6 ounces beer or wine
4 dashes Worcestershire sauce
  or soy sauce
1 dash Tabasco

- Cook roast in a 4-quart slow cooker on low for 10 to 12 hours or on high for 5 to 6 hours.

- Remove roast from pot. Clean pot.

- Remove meat from bone and chop into small pieces. Return to cooker; add remaining ingredients and cook on high for 2 or 3 hours. Serve on hamburger buns.

Yield: 8 generous servings

Barbara Hamlen

HAM & SPINACH CASSEROLE

10 to 12 slices bread
6 slices Old English sharp cheese
1 package frozen spinach, cooked
  and drained

3 slices country ham, cut in
  bite-size pieces
2¼ cups milk
4 eggs, beaten
½ teaspoon dry mustard

- Place half of bread slices on bottom of a greased 2-quart casserole dish. Layer cheese, spinach, and ham over bread; top with remaining bread slices.

- Combine milk and eggs and pour over all; allow to stand for 1 or 2 hours.

- Bake at 350° for 45 minutes.

Yield: 6 servings

Catherine Arnot

HOT MUSTARD

My husband's family always uses this mustard with meat.
Every time we sit down to dinner, he says "Where's the mustard?"

1 (2-ounce) can dry mustard   dash of salt
cider vinegar   1 cup sugar
2 eggs

- Empty can of mustard into a 1 cup measuring cup; fill cup with vinegar. Allow to stand for 1 hour.

- Beat eggs in top of double boiler; add salt, sugar, and mustard mixture.

- Cook over boiling water until thickened, stirring constantly. Store in refrigerator.

    Yield: 1½ cups

Sarah Eggleston

JACK BONE'S SAUCE

"This sauce was a favorite of Jack Bone,
famous lowcountry hog hunter and alligator wrestler."

2 cups apple cider vinegar   2 teaspoons chili powder
1 (15-ounce) can tomato paste   1 teaspoon dry mustard
1 cup chopped tomatoes   1 teaspoon garlic powder
½ cup minced onions   ¼ pound brown sugar
4 tablespoons black pepper   (or ¼ cup sugar substitute)
2 tablespoons red pepper flakes   1 tablespoon chopped sweet basil
1 teaspoon salt

- Combine all ingredients in a saucepan; simmer 1 hour.

    Yield: 4 cups

    Delicious on all meats, wild and domestic. Jack liked the sauce hot and sweet.

Steve Beattie

FAVORITE MEAT LOAF

2 pounds ground round	1 package dry onion soup mix
2 eggs	¾ cup ketchup
1 cup bread crumbs	4 strips bacon
1 bell pepper, finely chopped	1 can tomato soup

- Combine ground round and next 5 ingredients; mix well.
- Form into a loaf and place in a 10-inch iron skillet; cover meat loaf with bacon strips.
- Bake at 350° for 30 minutes.
- Pour tomato soup over meat loaf and bake 30 minutes longer.

Yield: 6 to 8 servings

Aimee Kornegay

GLAZED CORNED BEEF

3 pounds corned beef	4 tablespoons Dijon mustard
1 cup orange marmalade	4 tablespoons brown sugar

- Place corned beef in a large saucepan and cover with boiling water. Bring back to a boil, lower heat, cover partially, and simmer as slowly as possible for about 3 hours or until very tender.
- Combine marmalade, mustard, and sugar in a small bowl and mix well.
- Remove beef from pot and drain. Place beef on an ovenproof serving dish and pour marmalade mixture over, coating thoroughly.
- Bake at 350° for 30 minutes, or until glaze is crisp and brown. Serve hot or at room temperature.

Yield: 6 to 8 servings

Jesse T. Reese, Jr.

"For every beast of the forest is Mine,
the cattle on a thousand hills."
Psalm 50:10

VEGETABLES &
SIDE DISHES

VEGETABLES & SIDE DISHES

Harvard Beets
Broccoli Gratin
Broccoli Mold with Almonds
Broccoli & Onion Casserole
Curried Brussel Sprouts
Creamy Cauliflower
Celery Casserole
Lima Bean Casserole
Eggplant Parmesan
Shrimp-Stuffed Eggplant
Acorn Squash
Spinach & Wild Rice Casserole
Onion Jam "Kay"
Posh Squash
V.V.'s Favorite Squash Casserole
Squash Tarts
Baked Sweet Potato Sticks
Edisto Tomato Pie
Hot Stuffed Tomatoes
Broiled Tomatoes Mary

Marinated Tomatoes Edisto
Incredible Baked Beans
Catherine's Yellow Corn Pudding
Spoon Bread
Real Lowcountry Hopp'n' John
Vidalia Onion Deep Dish
Spinach Rice
Sweet Potato Soufflé
"Cotton Taters"
Caramel Sweet Potatoes
Potatoes & Onions Anna
Bean Salsa
Baked Pineapple Casserole
Curried Fruit
Spiced Grapes
Pear Chutney
Petey's Jerusalem Artichoke Relish
Hollandaise Sauce
Candied Cranberries
Okra Pilau
Spinach Fromage

"Honor the Lord from your wealth
and from the first of all your produce."
Proverbs 3:9

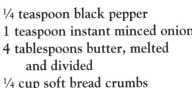

HARVARD BEETS

3 tablespoons sugar
3 tablespoons cider vinegar
1½ teaspoons cornstarch

1 bunch beets, cooked and sliced,
   or 1 can sliced beets

- Boil sugar, vinegar, and cornstarch together until clear. Add beets and heat over very low heat until heated thoroughly.

Yield: 4 servings

Frances Leitner

½ teaspoon powdered cloves may be added.

Mildred Ann Rodwell

BROCCOLI GRATIN

1 box frozen chopped broccoli
2 eggs, slightly beaten
1 teaspoon seasoned salt
¼ teaspoon steak sauce
1 cup dry cottage cheese
¼ teaspoon salt

¼ teaspoon black pepper
1 teaspoon instant minced onion
4 tablespoons butter, melted
   and divided
¼ cup soft bread crumbs

- Cook broccoli according to box directions. Drain.

- Mix broccoli with eggs and next 6 ingredients. Stir in 2 tablespoons butter. Place in a small baking dish. Mix remaining butter with bread crumbs and sprinkle on top.

- Bake at 350° for 30 minutes.

Yield: 4 to 6 servings

Gale Belser

BROCCOLI MOLD WITH ALMONDS

Delicious and different.

2 (10-ounce) boxes frozen
  chopped broccoli
3 tablespoons butter
3 tablespoons flour
¼ cup chicken broth
1 cup sour cream
⅓ cup minced green onions,
  tops and all

3 eggs, lightly beaten
¾ cup grated Swiss cheese
½ cup slivered almonds, toasted
1 teaspoon salt
½ teaspoon black pepper
½ teaspoon nutmeg

- Cook broccoli in 1 cup salted water until tender. Drain. Chop finely by hand.

- Melt butter in a skillet, blend in flour, add chicken broth and sour cream gradually. Stir in green onions and cook over low heat, stirring until thick and blended. Add eggs to sauce, blending well. Cook 1 minute, stirring constantly.

- Blend in cheese until melted. Add broccoli, almonds, salt, pepper, and nutmeg, mixing well. Spoon mixture into a 1-quart ring mold or 8 (5-ounce) custard cups.

- Bake at 350° in water bath for 50 minutes for a ring or 30 minutes for cups.

Yield: 6 to 8 servings

May be frozen before cooking. Defrost before baking.

Anges Messemer

BROCCOLI & ONION CASSEROLE

2 (10-ounce) boxes frozen
  broccoli florets
4 tablespoons margarine
2 tablespoons flour
1 cup milk
1 (3-ounce) package cream cheese

2 cups whole can medium onions
¼ teaspoons salt
black pepper to taste
1 cup soft bread crumbs
¼ cup Parmesan cheese

- Cook broccoli as directed on package and drain.

- Make a sauce of butter, flour, and milk stirring until sauce bubbles. Reduce heat. Cut cream cheese into small pieces and add to sauce, stirring until smooth. Add broccoli, onions, salt, and black pepper. Mix well. Place into a greased 1½-quart casserole.

- Bake at 350° for 20 minutes. Add bread crumbs to Parmesan mixing well. Sprinkle on top. Dot with butter and bake for an additional 20 minutes.

Yield: 10 servings

Gale Belser

CURRIED BRUSSELS SPROUTS

1 (10-ounce) box frozen Brussels
  sprouts
¼ cup mayonnaise

1 tablespoon Parmesan cheese
⅛ teaspoon celery seed
⅛ teaspoon curry powder

- Prepare Brussels sprouts according to package directions. Drain.

- Mix remaining ingredients in a medium sauce pan and add Brussels sprouts. Toss gently over low heat until hot.

Yield: 4 servings

Ramona Bosserman

171

CREAMY CAULIFLOWER

1 teaspoon salt, divided
2 tablespoons water
2 (10-ounce) boxes frozen
   cauliflower
1 tablespoon butter, softened
1 tablespoon flour
½ cup milk

1 cup small curd cottage cheese
½ cup grated cheddar cheese
1 tablespoon chopped pimento
⅛ teaspoon black pepper
½ cup crushed corn flakes
½ teaspoon paprika
½ teaspoon dill weed

- Place ½ teaspoon salt in a 2-quart microwave safe casserole. Add water and cauliflower. Microwave on high 14 to 16 minutes. Place in colander to drain.

- Blend butter and flour. Stir in milk, cottage cheese, cheddar cheese, and pimento. Microwave on high 6 minutes. Stir after 3 minutes until cheese melts and mixture thickens. Add remaining salt and pepper. Mix cauliflower gently into sauce. Sprinkle with corn flakes mixed with paprika and dill weed.

- Microwave on high 8 to 10 minutes until hot.

Yield: 6 servings

Gale Belser

CELERY CASSEROLE

2½ cups bite-size celery
2 tablespoons margarine
1 cup mushrooms
½ small bell pepper
1 (4-ounce) can pimento

1 (8-ounce) can sliced
   water chestnuts
1 can cream of mushroom soup
bread crumbs
paprika

- Sauté celery in butter until tender. Mix with mushrooms and next 4 ingredients. Place in a baking dish. Top with buttered bread crumbs and sprinkle with paprika.

- Bake at 325° for 20 minutes.

Yield: 4 to 6 servings

LIMA BEAN CASSEROLE

2 boxes frozen tiny lima beans
¼ cup butter, melted
1 teaspoon dry mustard

¾ teaspoon salt
2 teaspoons molasses
1 cup sour cream

- Mix all ingredients together and place in a prepared baking dish.
- Bake at 350° for 1 hour.

Yield: 8 servings

Catherine Arnot

EGGPLANT PARMESAN

2½ cups low fat spaghetti sauce
1 medium eggplant, peeled and cut
  into ½-inch slices

12 ounces mozzarella cheese,
  grated

- Spray a 13x9-inch baking dish with non-stick cooking spray. Pour ½ cup sauce on bottom of dish. Arrange ½ of eggplant slices over sauce. Top with ½ of mozzarella. Repeat with remaining eggplant and sauce. Cover with aluminum foil.
- Bake at 350° for 45 to 55 minutes. Top with remaining cheese and continue to bake, uncovered, until cheese melts.

Yield: 4 servings

Delicious, low-fat, and only 300 calories per serving.

Denise Driggers

Bless, O Lord, this food
to our use and us to thy service,
and make us ever mindful and responsive
to the needs of others.
In Jesus Christ's name we ask.
Amen.

SHRIMP-STUFFED EGGPLANT

2 medium eggplants
½ cup chopped onion
⅓ cup chopped celery
1 clove garlic, minced
1 tablespoon butter
1 pound shrimp, peeled

⅓ cup plus 2 tablespoons Italian
    seasoned bread crumbs
¼ teaspoon garlic powder
¼ teaspoon celery salt
⅛ teaspoon red pepper
1½ tablespoons butter

- Slice eggplants in half lengthwise. Remove pulp, leaving a ¼ to ½-inch shell. Chop pulp and set shells aside.

- Cook onion, celery, garlic, and eggplant pulp in butter over medium-high heat, stirring constantly, for 10 to 12 minutes or until tender. Add shrimp. Cook, stirring constantly, for 3 to 5 minutes or until shrimp turns pink. Remove from heat. Stir in ⅓ cup bread crumbs, garlic powder, celery salt, and red pepper.

- Place eggplant shells on a baking sheet. Spoon hot mixture into shells. Sprinkle with remaining bread crumbs and dot with butter.

- Bake at 350° for 20 to 25 minutes.

Yield: 4 servings

Bert Hatch

ACORN SQUASH

2 acorn squash
½ cup orange marmalade

½ cup margarine

- Cut squash in half and remove seeds.

- Bake at 350° for 45 minutes, cut-side down. Turn squash over. Spoon in mixture of marmalade and butter. Cook 15 minutes longer.

Yield: 4 servings

Gale Belser

SPINACH & WILD RICE CASSEROLE

Good dish to serve with game or fowl.

1 package white and wild rice
1 can beef broth
2 boxes frozen chopped spinach
1 (8-ounce) package cream
   cheese, softened
salt to taste

1 pound fresh mushrooms, sliced
3 tablespoons butter
1 (14½-ounce) can diced
   tomatoes, drained
4 slices bacon

- Cook rice as directed on package, substituting an equal amount of the beef broth for water. Set aside.

- Cook spinach, covered, until tender. Drain well and combine with cream cheese. Add salt and set aside.

- Sauté mushrooms in butter until just golden. Combine mushrooms and tomatoes.

- Grease a 2-quart casserole dish and layer half the rice, half the spinach mixture, and half the mushroom mixture. Repeat layers. Place bacon on top. Cover with foil.

- Bake at 350° for 40 minutes. Remove foil and place under broiler until bacon is crisp.

Yield: 6 to 8 servings

Van Leer Rowe

ONION JAM "KAY"

A perfect vegetable for roast duck, goose, or venison from Edisto Island!

1 pound red onions
1 liter of red wine

¼ pound sugar
2 tablespoons wine vinegar

- Chop onions, very fine, for 1 minute in a food processor.

- Mix onions and remaining ingredients together in a saucepan. Cook over medium heat until all liquid is absorbed by onions.

Yield: 4 servings

David Gibbons

175

POSH SQUASH ⊂⋈

People who don't like squash like this!

2 pounds yellow squash	1 cup grated cheddar or Parmesan
2 eggs	cheese
¼ cup bell pepper, chopped	salt and pepper to taste
¼ cup chopped green onions	buttered bread crumbs
1 cup mayonnaise	

- Slice squash, cut slices in quarters. Steam until tender and drain thoroughly.

- Beat eggs in a large bowl and add next 5 ingredients. Pour into a greased casserole dish and top with buttered bread crumbs.

- Bake at 350° for 30 minutes.

  Yield: 6 to 8 servings

Frances Guy

V.V.'S FAVORITE SQUASH CASSEROLE

1 pound summer squash, sliced	½ cup butter, melted and divided
½ cup grated sharp cheddar cheese	1 teaspoon salt
½ cup mayonnaise	dash of black pepper
2 tablespoons sugar	8 round buttery crackers, crumbled
1 egg, beaten	

- Cook squash in ½ cup water for 10 minutes. Drain. Add cheese, mayonnaise, sugar, egg, ¼ cup butter, salt and pepper. Mix well.

- Pour into a greased 2-quart baking dish. Cover with cracker crumbs which have been mixed with remaining ¼ cup butter.

- Bake at 400° for 20 minutes until bubbly.

  Yield: 6 to 8 servings

  Dress up with chopped pecans, if desired. Freezes well.

V.V. Thompson

SQUASH TARTS

2 pounds yellow squash
1 medium onion, chopped
½ cup butter
1 cup bacon bits

1 cup sour cream
tart shells
Parmesan cheese

- Cook squash and onion in boiling salted water until tender. Drain. In a bowl mix squash mixture with butter, bacon bits, and sour cream.

- Put into tart shells. Top with Parmesan cheese.

- Bake at 350° until hot and bubbly.

Yield: 4 to 6 servings

May be made ahead and frozen.

Cathy Richardson

BAKED SWEET POTATO STICKS

6 small sweet potatoes
1 tablespoon olive or canola oil

½ teaspoon paprika

- Slice potatoes into quarters, lengthwise.

- Mix together oil and paprika. Add potato sticks. Stir by hand to coat. Place on a greased baking sheet.

- Bake at 400° for 40 minutes.

Yield: 6 servings

Ed Camp

EDISTO TOMATO PIE

A delicious Southern favorite!

1 (9-inch) deep dish pie shell,
    prebaked at 375°for 10 minutes
5 large tomatoes, peeled and
    thickly sliced
½ teaspoon salt

½ teaspoon black pepper
3 teaspoons dried basil
garlic powder to taste
¾ cup mayonnaise
1¼ cups grated cheddar cheese

- Layer tomatoes in pie shell, sprinkling each layer with salt, pepper, basil, and garlic powder which have been combined.

- Combine mayonnaise and cheese; spread over tomatoes.

- Bake at 350° for 35 minutes or until golden brown and bubbly. Let stand 5 minutes before serving.

Yield: 6 to 8 servings

Wonderful served with shrimp and grits, butter beans, and everlasting slaw.

Aimee Kornegay

May add 1 large onion, chopped, and top with herb dressing mix.

Mary Crawford

178

HOT STUFFED TOMATOES

⅓ cup chopped green onions
1 cup celery, chopped
½ cup chopped bell pepper
2 tablespoons vegetable oil
1 (10-ounce) box frozen sliced okra
8 medium tomatoes

12 ounces hot bulk sausage
½ teaspoon basil
1 tablespoon parsley
½ teaspoon salt
bread crumbs

- Cook onions, celery, and bell pepper in oil until tender. Add okra and simmer 45 minutes, stirring often. Set aside.

- Scoop out tomatoes. Turn upside down on a paper towel and let drain. Chop pulp and add to okra mixture.

- Combine sausage with basil, parsley, and salt. Brown sausage and drain off fat. Stir into okra mixture. Spoon into tomato shells. Sprinkle with bread crumbs. Place in a shallow baking dish with a few tablespoons of water in the bottom of dish.

- Bake at 350° for 20 to 25 minutes.

Yield: 8 servings

Bo Lachicotte

BROILED TOMATOES MARY

1 cup sour cream
1 tablespoon flour
2 tablespoons chopped green onion
2 tablespoons chopped green chilies

½ teaspoon salt
¼ teaspoon black pepper
4 large tomatoes, sliced ½-inch thick
grated cheddar cheese

- Combine sour cream and flour, mixing well. Add onions, chilies, salt, and pepper; mix well.

- Spread on tomato slices and sprinkle with cheese.

- Broil 4 minutes.

Yield: 6 to 8 servings

Mary Crawford

MARINATED TOMATOES EDISTO

A summer treat!

3 large tomatoes, sliced
⅓ cup olive oil
¼ cup red wine vinegar
1 teaspoon salt
¼ teaspoon black pepper

½ clove garlic, crushed or
    ¼ teaspoon garlic powder
1 tablespoon chopped basil or
    1 teaspoon dried basil
2 tablespoon chopped onion

- Arrange tomatoes in a large shallow dish.

- Combine olive oil with remaining ingredients in a jar, cover tightly, and shake vigorously.

- Pour mixture over tomatoes, cover and marinate in refrigerator for several hours before serving.

Yield: 4 to 6 servings

Van Leer Rowe

INCREDIBLE BAKED BEANS

1 pound sausage
1 medium bell pepper,
    finely chopped
1 medium onion, chopped

3 cups canned baked beans
1 teaspoon prepared mustard
1 (12-ounce) can apricots, cut up
⅓ cup chili sauce

- Brown sausage, bell pepper, and onion. Set aside.

- Mix beans with remaining ingredients. Add to sausage mixture. Place in a 3-quart casserole.

- Bake at 350° for 30 minutes.

Yield: 6 to 8 servings

Linda Dennis

CATHERINE'S YELLOW CORN PUDDING

2 cups creamed corn, fresh or frozen
1½ tablespoons flour
4 tablespoons sugar
¼ teaspoon mace
red pepper to taste

salt to taste
4 eggs, beaten
¼ cup butter, melted
¾ cup milk

- Mix corn with flour and seasonings. Add eggs, butter, and milk.

- Pour mixture into a greased 1½-quart baking dish. Place in a water bath (pan with 1 inch of water) in the oven.

- Bake at 350° for 1 hour.

  Yield: 6 servings

Catherine Arnot

SPOON BREAD

Serve with any Southern meal!

1 cup self-rising corn meal
1 cup plain yogurt
1 (16-ounce) can cream style corn

4 eggs, beaten
½ cup corn oil

- Combine corn meal, yogurt, corn, and eggs in a bowl; stir well. Set aside.

- Pour oil into a 1½-quart casserole dish; place in a 425° oven until oil is very hot.

- Pour hot oil into corn meal mixture; mix well and return to casserole dish.

- Bake at 350° for 30 minutes or until golden brown.

  Yield: 6 to 8 servings

  Spoon bread may not be made ahead because it will fall; prepare for immediate serving.

  May add jalapeño peppers and cheese to corn meal mixture before baking.

Mary Dean Richards

REAL LOWCOUNTRY HOPP'N' JOHN

1 cup cow peas
1 ham hock
1 large onion, chopped

4 cups water
1 cup washed raw rice

- Boil peas, ham hock, and onion in water until peas are almost done. Put 1 cup pea liquid with rice in a rice steamer or the top of a double boiler pot. Add drained peas, ham hock (skin and fat removed, meat diced), and onion.

- Steam 1 hour. After steaming 20 minutes, fluff with a fork.

Yield: 4 to 6 servings

2 slices lean Canadian bacon plus one packet ham bouillon substituted for ham hock cuts fat to almost zero.

Virginia Guerard

VIDALIA ONION DEEP DISH

1⅛ cups rice
½ cup butter, melted
6 medium Vidalia onions,
   chopped
1⅛ cup grated Swiss cheese

1 cup heavy cream
2 tablespoons parsley, minced
salt and pepper to taste
paprika

- Cook rice in boiling water for 5 minutes. Drain.

- Sauté onions in butter until tender. Set aside.

- Mix cream and cheese. Add parsley, salt, and black pepper. Mix cream mixture with onions and rice. Pour into a greased 13x9x2-inch baking dish. Sprinkle with paprika.

- Bake at 325° for 1 hour.

Yield: 10 to 12 servings

Veda Godwin

SPINACH RICE

1 cup rice, cooked and cooled
½ cup Italian dressing
1 tablespoon soy sauce
½ teaspoon sugar
2 cups fresh spinach, cut in strips

½ cup sliced celery
½ cup chopped green onions
   with tops
⅓ cup bacon, fried and chopped

• Mix rice with Italian dressing, soy sauce, and sugar. Cover and chill overnight.

• Combine rice mixture with remaining ingredients. Serve cold or warm.

Yield: 4 to 6 servings

Judy Inman

SWEET POTATO SOUFFLÉ

Everyone always asks for seconds!

4 cups sweet potatoes, cooked
¼ cup butter, melted
½ cup evaporated milk

3 eggs, beaten
1 cup sugar
¼ teaspoon salt

• Place potatoes in bowl of a food processor and process until almost smooth. Add butter and next 4 ingredients and process until completely smooth. Pour into a greased baking dish.

• Prepare topping. Sprinkle on top of the sweet potato mixture.

• Bake at 350° for 30 minutes.

TOPPING

¼ cup self-rising flour
2 tablespoons butter, melted

½ cup light brown sugar, packed
½ cup pecans, chopped

• Blend flour, butter, sugar, and pecans using a fork until coarse, crumb-like mixture.

Yield: 6 to 8 servings

May double topping recipe to make even better.

Van Leer Rowe

"COTTON TATERS"

1 (32-ounce) box frozen hash
   browns, thawed 30 minutes
1 (16-ounce) carton sour cream
1 cup chopped onion
1 can cream of chicken soup

½ cup butter, melted
2½ cups grated sharp
   cheddar cheese
salt and pepper

- Mix all ingredients and place into 2 greased 13x9x2-inch casserole dish.

- Bake at 350° for 1 hour.

Yield: 10 to 12 servings

Cotton Richardson

Substitute cream of mushroom soup for cream of chicken and top with round buttery cracker crumbs mixed with butter. Bake at 350° for 45 minutes. Freezes well.

CARAMEL SWEET POTATOES

6 sweet potatoes, peeled and sliced
1 box light brown sugar

½ pint heavy cream

- Place potatoes in a greased 3-quart casserole and cover with sugar. Pour cream over top of potatoes and sugar.

- Bake at 375° for 1 hour. Check after 30 minutes, if potatoes on top are dry, spoon juice over top and continue to bake. Let sit for 15 minutes before serving.

Yield: 6 to 8 servings

Martha Whetstone

POTATOES & ONIONS ANNA

¾ teaspoon salt
¼ teaspoon white pepper
4 pounds potatoes, thinly sliced

4 large onions, thinly sliced
½ cup butter, divided
⅓ cup Parmesan cheese

- Combine salt and pepper. Layer ⅓ potatoes and then ⅓ onions. Sprinkle with ⅓ salt mixture and dot with ⅓ butter in a greased 2-quart shallow baking dish. Repeat twice.

- Bake, covered, at 350° for 45 minutes. Uncover and bake until lightly browned. Sprinkle with Parmesan and bake 5 minutes or until cheese lightly browns.

Yield: 8 servings

Randolph Berretta

BEAN SALSA

1 cup cooked black beans, rinsed
1 cup cooked navy beans, rinsed
1 small tomato, diced
½ red onion, chopped
½ bell pepper, chopped
3 tablespoons chopped parsley
 or cilantro

½ yellow bell pepper, chopped
2 tablespoons olive oil
3 tablespoons wine vinegar
1 teaspoon sugar
salt and pepper to taste
¼ hot pepper (optional)
few drops of Tabasco (optional)

- Mix all ingredients in a bowl. Cover. Place in refrigerator for at least 4 hours. Stir and serve.

Yield: 3 cups

This is especially nice with Mexican food or grilled food.

Lisa Barclay

BAKED PINEAPPLE CASSEROLE

This is wonderful served with poultry, pork, or game.

1 (16-ounce) can pineapple chunks, drained and juice reserved
½ cup sugar
3 tablespoons flour

1 cup grated cheddar cheese
¼ cup margarine, melted
½ cup crushed round buttery crackers

- Mix sugar, flour, and pineapple juice until smooth. Add pineapple chunks and cheese. Toss until well coated. Pour into a greased 1½-quart casserole dish.

- Mix cracker crumbs with margarine and sprinkle on top.

- Bake at 325° for 20 to 25 minutes.

Yield: 4 to 6 servings

Mary Alice Beck
Veda Godwin

CURRIED FRUIT

Great with game, pork, or poultry!

1 (29-ounce) can peach halves
1 (20-ounce) can pineapples slices
1 (29-ounce) can pear halves
1 (10-ounce) jar maraschino cherries

¾ cup light brown sugar, packed
4 teaspoons curry powder
⅓ cup butter, melted

- Drain fruits and arrange in baking dish. Dot with cherries.

- Mix brown sugar and curry powder with butter. Spoon over fruit.

- Bake at 350° for 1 hour.

Yield: 10 servings

Exact amount or type of fruit is not important. Use a combination you enjoy!

Timmy Dorn, Ebby Hatch, Judy Tomlin

SPICED GRAPES

Wonderful with venison!

5 pounds grapes (thin-skinned purple grapes)	1 tablespoon cinnamon
1 cup vinegar	1 tablespoon cloves
3 pounds sugar	1 tablespoon allspice
	1 tablespoon nutmeg

- Remove skins of grapes and set aside.

- Combine pulp and vinegar in a large saucepan and cook until soft.

- Press mixture through a sieve to separate from seeds.

- Combine pulp and remaining ingredients and boil for 20 minutes. Spoon into sterilized jars and seal.

Yield: 6 pints

Do not double!!!!

Betty Belser

PEAR CHUTNEY

10 cups pears, peeled, cored, and chopped	2 lemons, thinly sliced
3 pounds brown sugar (light or dark)	1-2 cloves garlic
1 quart vinegar	3 tablespoons mustard seed
1 pound raisins (golden or purple)	2 tablespoons chili powder
	3 teaspoons salt
	1 pound ginger preserves

- Soak pears overnight in sugar.

- Combine remaining ingredients except preserves in a large saucepan and boil until pears are tender.

- Remove pears from syrup and continue to boil until syrup thickens.

- Return pears to syrup, add preserves, and mix well. Spoon chutney into sterilized jars and seal.

Yield: 6 pints

Gale Belser

PETEY'S JERUSALEM ARTICHOKE RELISH

This recipe has long been a family favorite — well worth the time and effort!

3 quarts Jerusalem artichokes,
  scrubbed
1 quart onions
3 bell peppers
2 red bell peppers

1 cauliflower, broken into
  tiny florets
1 gallon water
1 pint salt

- Chop artichokes, onions, and peppers coarsely in a food processor.
- Mix with remaining ingredients; cover and let stand 24 hours.
- Pour into a colander and drain well.
- Prepare sauce. Add vegetables, stir well; bring to a boil; seal in sterile jars while hot.

SAUCE

1 cup flour
8 tablespoons dry mustard
1 tablespoon turmeric
4 tablespoons mustard seed

8 tablespoons celery seed
4 cups sugar
½ gallon vinegar, divided

- Mix all dry ingredients in a large saucepan; add vinegar (about 1 cup) to make a paste.
- Heat remaining vinegar in another saucepan; pour over mustard paste.
- Return to heat and boil until sauce thickens, stirring constantly.

  Yield: 13 pints

  Excellent accompaniment for any green vegetable, especially collards.

  Aimee Nelson

May God be
within us to refresh us,
around us to protect us,
before us to guide us,
above us to bless us,
beneath us to support us;
Who liveth and reigneth, one God, world within end.

Amen.

HOLLANDAISE SAUCE

This Hollandaise sauce never fails!

4 egg yolks
2 tablespoons fresh lemon juice
½ cup butter, divided into 3 pieces

¼ teaspoon salt
dash of cayenne
¼ cup boiling water

- Beat egg yolks and lemon juice in top of a double boiler.

- Place over simmering water and add 1 piece of butter, stirring constantly until thickening begins.

- Remove from heat; add second piece of butter and stir rapidly. Add third piece of butter and stir until mixture is completely blended. Add salt, cayenne, and water.

- Return to double boiler and stir until thickened.

Yield: 1 cup

Cook sauce over a small amount of slowly simmering water. Do not let water boil. May be refrigerated and reheated.

Van Leer Rowe

CANDIED CRANBERRIES

A real treat!

4 cups cranberries
3 cups sugar
1 cup water

¼ teaspoon soda
¼ teaspoon salt

- Mix all ingredients in a heavy saucepan. Bring to a boil. Turn to low and cook covered 15 to 20 minutes. Do not remove cover until cool.

Yield: 1 quart

Missy Camp

OKRA PILAU

1½ cups rice	1 teaspoon soy sauce
1½ cups water	¼ teaspoon black pepper
10 bacon slices, reserve drippings	¼ teaspoon garlic salt
1 medium onion, chopped	¼ teaspoon salt
1 medium bell pepper, chopped	dash of seasoning salt
2 stalks celery, diced	mushrooms (optional)
3 cups okra, chopped	

- Cook rice in rice steamer

- Fry bacon until crisp. Drain and crumble. Sauté onion, bell pepper, and celery in drippings for 2 minutes, remove. Add okra and cook until brown. Add all to rice just before rice is done. Add soy sauce and next 4 ingredients as rice finishes cooking. Stir bacon in last.

Yield: 6 servings

Veda Godwin

SPINACH FROMAGE

3 tablespoons butter or margarine	1½ cups soft bread crumbs
3 tablespoons flour	3 eggs, beaten
1½ cups milk	1½ teaspoons salt
½ cup grated cheddar cheese	dash of black pepper
1 (10-ounce) box frozen chopped spinach	¼ teaspoon nutmeg

- Melt butter and add flour. Mix well. Gradually add milk and cook slowly until thickened. Add cheese and blend.

- Cut frozen spinach into pieces. Put in a medium casserole dish and add bread crumbs and next 4 ingredients. Pour cream sauce over mixture.

- Bake at 350° for 1 hour.

Yield: 4 servings

Frances Richardson

SALADS &
SALAD
DRESSINGS

SALADS & SALAD DRESSINGS

Elegant Crab Salad
Grandmother Belser's Shrimp
    & Potato Salad
Prause's Shrimp Salad
Shrimp-Pasta Salad
Seafood Aspic
Edisto Chicken Salad
Captain John's Wahoo Salad
Salad of Black Beans,
    Hearts of Palm, & Corn
Curried Rice & Chicken Salad
Tomato Aspic
Chicken Pasta Salad
Ruby Cranberry Salad
Asparagus Salad
Petey's Pasta Salad
Sweet 'n' Sour Broccoli Salad
Blue Cheese Potato Salad
Dreamy Apricot Salad

Cold Curried Rice Salad
Layered Overnight Salad
Mandarin Orange Salad
French Dressing
Blue Cheese Dressing
Mexican Village Dressing
Thousand Island Dressing
Tomato Soup Salad Dressing
Belle's Salad Dressing
Honey-Mustard Dressing
Good Salad Dressing
Homemade Fat Free Ranch
    Salad Dressing
Honey Dijon Dressing
Melba's Mayonnaise
Poppy Seed Dressing
Fruit Dressing or Dip
Everlasting Cole Slaw
Sarah's Salad Dressing

"Then God said, 'Behold I have given you
every plant yielding seed
that is on the surface of all the earth,
and every tree which has fruit yielding seed;
and it shall be food for you'."
Genesis 1:29

ELEGANT CRAB SALAD

A great buffet dish!

4 cups backfin crabmeat
1 cup finely chopped celery
3 tablespoons finely chopped onion
½ cup mayonnaise
3 hard-boiled eggs, finely chopped
2 tablespoons minced parsley

2 tablespoons lemon juice
2 tablespoons Dijon mustard
dash of Worcestershire sauce
dash of black pepper
shredded lettuce
paprika

- Combine crabmeat, celery, and onion.

- Mix together remaining ingredients, except lettuce and paprika.

- Combine crabmeat with dressing and chill for 30 minutes or longer.

- Line salad bowl with shredded lettuce, add salad, and sprinkle lightly with paprika.

Yield: 8 to 10 servings

Shrimp or lobster may be substituted for crabmeat

Aimee Kornegay

GRANDMOTHER BELSER'S SHRIMP & POTATO SALAD

Excellent for a luncheon!

3 pounds shrimp, cooked
    and peeled
4-5 large potatoes, cooked
    and cubed
3 hard-boiled eggs, chopped

1 cup chopped celery
1 small onion, finely chopped
salt and pepper to taste
capers (optional)
mayonnaise to bind

- Combine shrimp, potatoes, eggs, celery, and onion.

- Add mayonnaise and seasonings. Chill and serve.

Yield: 12 servings

Gale Belser

193

PRAUSE'S SHRIMP SALAD

Wonderful luncheon fare!

3 pounds shrimp, cooked, peeled, and coarsely chopped
1 bell pepper, finely chopped
1 red bell pepper, finely chopped
1 yellow bell pepper, finely chopped
3 stalks celery, chopped

2 green onions, chopped
1 tablespoon lemon juice
1 teaspoon prepared mustard
1 teaspoon Worcestershire sauce
Tabasco to taste
salt and pepper to taste
1 cup mayonnaise

- Combine all ingredients; mix well.
- Serve on a bed of lettuce.

  Yield: 6 to 8 servings

Walter Prause

SHRIMP-PASTA SALAD

2 cups cooked green noodles
2 cups cooked white noodles
1 pound cooked whole shrimp

¼ cup sliced ripe olives
1 small can sliced mushrooms
2-3 ounces feta cheese

- Combine ingredients.
- Prepare dressing. Pour over salad and toss.
- Serve with sliced tomatoes, bell pepper rings, and hard-boiled eggs, quartered.

DRESSING

1 tablespoon tarragon vinegar
½ cup olive oil
1 clove garlic, minced

1-2 teaspoons fresh chives
fresh parsley
2-3 teaspoons capers

- Mix all ingredients well.

  Yield: 4 to 6 servings

Mary Crawford

SEAFOOD ASPIC

Great dish for a summer lunch!

1 (10.5-ounce) can tomato soup
1 (8-ounce) package cream cheese
2 envelopes plain gelatin
½ cup cold water
¾ pound medium shrimp, cooked, peeled, and chopped into thirds
½ cup celery, finely chopped

1 small onion, finely chopped
½ cup bell pepper, chopped
1 cup Hellmann's® mayonnaise
dash of Tabasco
dash of Worcestershire sauce
Jane's Krazy Mixed-Up Salt®
    to taste

- Heat soup in top of a double boiler and add cream cheese.

- Mix gelatin with water and add to soup mixture. Remove from heat.

- Add shrimp and remaining 7 ingredients, mixing well. Pour into a greased 8x8x2-inch glass dish.

- Refrigerate until firm. Serve on a bed of lettuce and garnish with lemon wedges.

Yield: 8 to 10 servings

Walton Salley

EDISTO CHICKEN SALAD

This is good basic chicken salad!

2 cups chicken, diced
1 cup celery, chopped
¾ cup mayonnaise

2 tablespoons Durkee's® dressing
salt and pepper to taste
lettuce

- Combine chicken with next 4 ingredients, mixing well.

- Serve in lettuce cups.

Yield: 4 servings

May add some of the following: olives, pineapple, nuts, green grapes, pickles, shrimp, Mandarin oranges.

Tag Wylie

CAPTAIN JOHN'S WAHOO SALAD

Just wonderful!

2 pounds "white" Wahoo, dressed
  and cut into ¼-inch slices
1 lemon, divided
salt and pepper to taste
cayenne to taste

1 cup finely chopped celery
½ cup chopped leek
1½ cups mayonnaise
2 tablespoons mustard
2 tablespoons Worcestershire sauce

- Boil water and ½ lemon in a large saucepan; add Wahoo and cook until fish flakes. Just a few minutes! Drain and let cool.

- Flake fish and season with salt, pepper, and cayenne.

- Combine next 5 ingredients and remaining lemon juice; mix well and fold in Wahoo.

- Chill for several hours before serving.

Yield: 10 servings

May chop very, very fine and serve as a spread for crackers.

John Kornegay

SALAD OF BLACK BEANS, HEARTS OF PALM, & CORN

1 (16-ounce) can black beans,
  rinsed and drained
1 (10-ounce) package frozen corn,
  thawed and drained
1 (7½-ounce) can hearts of palm,
  drained and cut into
  ¼-inch rounds
2 large tomatoes, seeded and diced

½ red onion, minced
½ cup chopped fresh cilantro
¼ cup olive oil
4 tablespoons fresh lime juice
1 teaspoon ground coriander
  (optional)
salt and pepper to taste

- Combine all ingredients in a medium-size bowl and cover.

- Refrigerate overnight.

Yield: 4 to 6 servings

Mary Margaret Calk

CURRIED RICE & CHICKEN SALAD

Wonderful summer dish!

1⅓ cups rice, uncooked	½ teaspoon salt
2 chicken bouillon cubes	½ teaspoon pepper
2 tablespoons butter	4 tablespoons raisins
2 tablespoons curry powder	½ cup cashews
2 cups chicken, cooked, diced,	1 cup artichoke hearts
and chilled	1 medium onion, chopped

- Cook rice with bouillon cubes, butter, and curry. Chill.
- Combine with remaining ingredients and mix well.
- Prepare dressing; pour on salad mixture and mix.

DRESSING

1 cup mayonnaise	½ teaspoon curry powder
1 tablespoon lemon juice	

Yield: 8 servings

Green seedless grapes, chopped apples, pecans, or walnuts may be substituted or any ingredients you desire.

Jackie Adams

TOMATO ASPIC

1 package lemon jello	1 tablespoon vinegar
1½ cups hot water	garlic salt to taste
1 (8-ounce) can tomato soup	celery salt to taste
1 tablespoon prepared horseradish	

- Dissolve jello in hot water; add remaining ingredients and mix well.
- Pour into a mold and chill until set.

Yield: 6 servings

Frances Richardson

CHICKEN PASTA SALAD

Summer delight!

10 boneless chicken breasts, cooked
   and cut into bite-size pieces
1 pound medium noodles, cooked
5-6 stalks celery, finely chopped
1 bell pepper, chopped

2 jars chopped pimentos
1 onion, finely chopped
1 cup broccoli florets, cut small
½-1 cup parsley, chopped
toasted almonds for garnish

- Combine all ingredients and toss.

- Prepare dressing; pour over chicken and vegetables and toss.

- Refrigerate overnight. Garnish with toasted almonds and serve.

DRESSING

1½ cups salad oil
½ cup salad vinegar
1½ cups mayonnaise

1 tablespoon Creole seasoning
3 tablespoons lemon juice

- Mix ingredients with a wire whisk.

  Yield: 10 to 12 servings

Vangie Summers

RUBY CRANBERRY SALAD

2 (3-ounce) packages cherry jello
2 cups boiling water
1 cup cold water
2 tablespoons lemon juice

1 (16-ounce) jellied cranberry sauce
1 cup unsweetened cherries
½ cup chopped walnuts

- Dissolve jello in boiling water; stir in cold water and lemon juice.

- Chill until thick; fold in sauce, cherries, and nuts.

- Chill until congealed.

  *Whole cranberry sauce may be used if puréed in a food processor.
  Whisk in after mixture thickens.*

Mary Sue Ellis

ASPARAGUS SALAD

Pretty for a Christmas buffet!

2 envelopes unflavored gelatin
½ cup cold water
¾ cup sugar
1 cup boiling water
1 (2-ounce) jar chopped
    pimento, drained
1 cup finely chopped celery
½ cup finely chopped pecans

1½ teaspoons salt
1 teaspoon Worcestershire sauce
juice of 1 lemon
juice of 1 small onion
½ cup salad vinegar
1 cup asparagus juice
2 (8½-ounce) cans asparagus tips,
    reserve juice

- Dissolve gelatin in cold water. Dissolve sugar in boiling water.

- Combine all ingredients, except asparagus. Pour into a container and refrigerate until partially congealed.

- Pour ½ of mixture into a wet mold; place asparagus tips on top and cover with remaining mixture. Chill.

Yield: 10 to 12 servings

Aimee Kornegay

PETEY'S PASTA SALAD

1 pound tricolor spiral pasta, al
    dente (7 minutes) and drained
1½ cups Parmesan cheese, divided
8 stalks celery, sliced
½ pound carrots, thinly sliced
1 (2¼-ounce) can sliced ripe olives

½ cup chopped parsley
1 envelope dry Italian seasoned
    dressing mix
½ cup olive oil
½ cup white Balsamic vinegar

- Combine pasta and 1 cup Parmesan in a large bowl and toss; add next 4 ingredients and toss.

- Combine dressing mix, oil, and vinegar; whisk. Pour over pasta mixture; toss.

- Chill overnight for best flavor. Sprinkle with remaining Parmesan before serving.

May add any vegetables, shrimp, chicken, etc.

Aimee Nelson

SWEET 'N' SOUR BROCCOLI SALAD

1 bunch broccoli, cut into
small pieces
½ cup chopped red onion

½ cup raisins
½ pound bacon, cooked, drained,
and crumbled

- Combine all ingredients and toss.

- Prepare dressing; pour over salad.

- Refrigerate overnight.

DRESSING

1 cup mayonnaise
2 tablespoons red wine vinegar

¼ cup sugar

- Combine all ingredients; blend until smooth.

Yield: 8 to 10 servings

Grace Woodhead

*1 red apple, diced; sliced almonds, toasted; ½ pound sharp
cheese, grated; 1 red bell pepper, chopped.*

Mary Alice Beck, Mary Crawford, Ellie Howard

BLUE CHEESE POTATO SALAD

A flavorful new twist to the all-American potato salad!

2½ pounds unpeeled red potatoes
¼ cup dry white wine
salt and pepper to taste
½ cup mayonnaise
½ cup sour cream

1½ tablespoons Dijon mustard
1½ tablespoons cider vinegar
4 ounces Blue cheese, crumbled
3 green onions, finely chopped
1 cup coarsely chopped celery

- Boil potatoes until tender; drain and cool to room temperature.

- Cut into bite-size pieces and place in a large bowl. Add wine, salt, and pepper. Let stand until wine is absorbed.

- Combine mayonnaise and next 6 ingredients. Add to potatoes and stir well.

- Let stand at room temperature 30 minutes before serving.

Yield: 6 to 8 servings

DREAMY APRICOT SALAD

2 (3-ounce) packages apricot or
  lemon jello
⅔ cup water
2 (20-ounce) cans crushed
  pineapple, undrained

1 (14-ounce) can sweetened
  condensed milk
1 (8-ounce) package cream
  cheese, softened
1½ cups chopped pecans

- Combine jello and water in small saucepan; bring to a boil, stirring to dissolve jello.

- Remove from heat and stir in fruit. Set aside to cool.

- Combine cheese and milk, beating until smooth. Stir in jello mixture and nuts.

- Pour into a 9-cup mold and chill until firm.

Yield: 16 servings

Selina Lyman

COLD CURRIED RICE SALAD

4 cups chicken broth
2 cups rice, uncooked
½ teaspoon turmeric
½ tablespoon candied ginger, minced
2 tablespoons curry powder
¼ cup vegetable oil
½ cup fresh lemon juice

salt and pepper to taste
½ cup chopped bell pepper
½ cup slivered almonds, toasted
½ cup dark raisins
½ cup golden raisins
2½ tablespoons sour cream
2½ tablespoons mayonnaise

- Combine broth, rice, turmeric, ginger, and curry in a large saucepan and bring to a boil. Reduce heat to low; cover and simmer until rice is tender and liquid is absorbed (about 30 minutes).

- Transfer to a large bowl; add oil and lemon juice. Toss well and season with salt and pepper. Cover tightly and refrigerate overnight.

- Add pepper, almonds, and raisins; toss gently. Stir in sour cream and mayonnaise.

- Refrigerate until ready to serve.

Yield: 8 to 10 servings

Gale Belser

LAYERED OVERNIGHT SALAD

1 head lettuce, shredded
1 (1-pound) package fresh
  spinach, washed and trimmed
½ teaspoon salt
½ teaspoon sugar
⅛ teaspoon black pepper
6 hard-boiled eggs, sliced

1 pound bacon, cooked crisp
  and crumbled
2 (10-ounce) packages frozen
  peas, thawed and divided
¾ cup sliced red or green onions
2 cups grated Swiss cheese, divided
1¼ cups mayonnaise

- Place half of lettuce and half of spinach in a large bowl. Sprinkle with salt, sugar, and pepper.

- Add layers of eggs, bacon, 1 package peas, onions, remaining lettuce, spinach, peas, and 1 cup cheese.

- Spread mayonnaise evenly over top and sprinkle with remaining cheese.

- Cover tightly with plastic wrap and refrigerate overnight.

- Toss just before serving or serve by digging deep through all the layers for each serving.

Yield: 16-20 servings

May be cut in half if desired.

Joan Foxworth

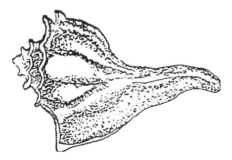

MANDARIN ORANGE SALAD

Wonderful for Thanksgiving!

2 small packages orange jello
2 cups boiling water
1 small can frozen orange juice
1 small can crushed pineapple,
    reserve ½ juice

3 cans mandarin oranges,
    drained and soaked in
    ½ cup vodka, divided

- Dissolve jello in water; add orange juice and stir.

- Add pineapple, reserved juice, two-thirds oranges, and ¼ cup vodka. Pour into a 13x9x2-inch glass dish and congeal.

- Prepare topping; spread on top of congealed mixture and garnish with remaining orange slices.

TOPPING

1 package instant lemon pudding
1 cup milk

1 (8-ounce) carton frozen
    whipped topping, thawed

- Mix pudding and milk. Add topping and blend.

Yield: 16 servings

Doris Gramling

FRENCH DRESSING

1 cup oil
½ cup vinegar
1 cup ketchup
½ cup sugar
2 teaspoons paprika

2 teaspoons salt
¼ teaspoon black pepper
¼ teaspoon garlic powder
¼ teaspoon celery seed

- Mix all ingredients and blend thoroughly. Store in refrigerator.

Yield: 3 cups

Excellent on salad of rice, green peas, slivered almonds, and chopped olives.

Frances Richardson

BLUE CHEESE DRESSING

2 ounces Blue cheese crumbles
1 cup mayonnaise

¼ cup lemon juice
¼ teaspoon garlic powder

- Mix all ingredients by hand in a small bowl; add additional lemon juice to thin, if desired.
- Store in refrigerator for 24 hours for better flavor.
- Mix well before serving as the dressing will separate. Serve at room temperature.

Yield: 1¼ cups

Will keep 3 to 4 weeks in refrigerator.

Cindy Lenz

MEXICAN VILLAGE DRESSING

½ cup crumbled blue cheese
1 cup oil
½ teaspoon salt
1 teaspoon black pepper
1 tablespoon Worcestershire sauce

2 tablespoons olive oil
1 raw egg
4 tablespoons lemon juice
3 cloves garlic

- Combine all ingredients in a blender; blend until mixed well. Store in refrigerator.

Yield: 1¼ cups

Bo Lachicotte

THOUSAND ISLAND DRESSING

2 cups mayonnaise
2 tablespoons sweet pickle relish
1 teaspoon vinegar

4 teaspoons sugar
3 tablespoons chili sauce

- Mix all ingredients and blend thoroughly. Store in refrigerator.

Yield: 2 cups

For variety, add 1 hard boiled egg, chopped.

Frances Richardson

TOMATO SOUP SALAD DRESSING

Excellent!

1 cup salad oil
1 cup vinegar
1 cup sugar
1 can tomato soup
1 tablespoon salt

1 teaspoon grated onion
1 clove garlic, peeled
1 tablespoon Worcestershire sauce
1 teaspoon lemon juice

- Combine all ingredients in a jar and shake well. Store in refrigerator.

  Yield: 3½ cups

Joan Foxworth

BELLE'S SALAD DRESSING

1 (11½-ounce) can tomato juice
1 cup vinegar
½ cup oil
¼ cup sugar

1 small onion, chopped
2 teaspoons salt
1 teaspoon black pepper
¼ teaspoon paprika

- Combine all ingredients in a quart jar and shake well. Store in refrigerator.

  Yield: 2½ cups

Belle Palmer

HONEY-MUSTARD DRESSING

¼ bunch parsley, chopped
1 small onion, chopped
4 tablespoons clear
  South Carolina honey

½ cup white vinegar
4 tablespoons Dijon mustard
¾ cup sunflower oil

- Combine all ingredients in a salad bowl and whisk to mix. Add greens of choice and toss.

  Yield: 2 cups

David Gibbons

GOOD SALAD DRESSING

½ cup olive oil
2 tablespoons red wine vinegar
½-1 teaspoon salad herbs
½-1 teaspoon salad seasonings
    for vinaigrette

1 clove garlic, minced
1 tablespoon Dijon mustard
1 tablespoon honey

- Mix all ingredients and pour into a jar. Store in refrigerator. Shake well before using.

- To serve: put dressing (1 tablespoon for 2 servings) in bottom of a salad bowl. Put greens on top and toss.

Yield: ¾ cup

Anne and Tom Peterson

HOMEMADE FAT FREE
RANCH SALAD DRESSING

1 cup fat free mayonnaise
1 cup buttermilk
2 tablespoons finely chopped
    green onion tops
¼ teaspoon onion powder
2 teaspoons minced parsley

¼ teaspoon garlic powder
¼ teaspoon paprika
⅛ teaspoon cayenne
¼ teaspoon salt
¼ teaspoon black pepper

- Combine all ingredients in a small container and mix well. Store in refrigerator.

Yield: 2 cups

Denise Driggers

207

HONEY DIJON DRESSING

1 cup mayonnaise
¼ cup Dijon mustard
¼ cup oil
¼ cup honey

⅛ teaspoon cider vinegar
½ teaspoon minced garlic
pinch of red pepper

- Mix all ingredients. Store in refrigerator.

Yield: 1½ cups

My wife makes this with low fat mayonnaise and olive oil — I still use it!

Cotton Richardson

MELBA'S MAYONNAISE

Lucious and versatile and ready in minutes!

3 egg yolks
¼ teaspoon dry mustard
½ teaspoon salt
1 teaspoon lemon juice, divided

½ teaspoon vinegar
2 cups salad or olive oil
paprika (optional)

- Chill all utensils and oil in freezer.

- Beat yolks until thick and sticky, about 1 to 1½ minutes. Add mustard, salt, ½ teaspoon lemon juice, and vinegar; beat again.

- Add chilled oil, drop by drop, until ½ cup has been added, constantly beating. It will be thick. Add remaining oil mixing until very thick; add remaining lemon juice and paprika. Store in air-tight container in refrigerator.

Yield: 2 cups

Ellie Howard

POPPY SEED DRESSING

Especially good on grapefruit and avocado salad!

¾ cup sugar
¼ teaspoon salt
1½ tablespoons grated onion
1½ tablespoons poppy seeds

1 teaspoon dry mustard
½ cup vinegar
1 cup salad oil

- Mix together sugar and salt; add onion, poppy seed, mustard, and vinegar, blending well. Slowly whisk in oil. Store in refrigerator.

  Yield: 1¾ cups

  Serve on fruit salad or spinach salad with mandarin oranges and sliced red onions.

  Gale Belser
  Ann Cowsert

FRUIT DRESSING OR DIP

1 (8-ounce) package cream
    cheese, softened
1 (8-ounce) carton sour cream

⅓ cup orange marmalade
2 tablespoons brown sugar

- Combine all ingredients and mix well.

  Yield: 2½ cups

  Mary Ella Hackett

EVERLASTING COLE SLAW

Our picnics always include this tasty salad!

1 head cabbage, shredded   1 bell pepper, shredded
1 onion, shredded

- Combine cabbage, onion, and pepper in a large bowl.
- Prepare dressing; pour over salad mixture; allow to stand 1 hour. Do not stir.
- Mix well and refrigerate for 24 hours before serving.

DRESSING

1 cup cider or red wine vinegar   ½ teaspoon garlic powder
½ cup olive oil   1 teaspoon dry mustard
½ cup sugar   1 teaspoon celery seed
1 teaspoon salt

- Combine all ingredients in a saucepan and bring to a boil.

Yield: 10 servings

May add red bell pepper for flavor and color.

Linda Dennis, Joan Foxworth, Aimee Nelson

SARAH'S SALAD DRESSING

¼ package Blue cheese crumbles   1 cup oil
1 tablespoon salt   ½ cup vinegar
1 tablespoon garlic salt   1 tablespoon paprika
½ teaspoon black pepper

- Combine all ingredients in a jar and shake well. Store in refrigerator.

Yield: 1½ cups

Bo Lachicotte

BREADS, MUFFINS, BISCUITS

'Pon Top Edisto

BREADS, MUFFINS, BISCUITS

Pumpkin Bread
Strawberry Bread
Carrot Loaf
Sour Cream Muffins
Zucchini Bread
Lemon-Raspberry Muffins
Bran Muffins
Sallie's Biscuits
Blueberry Muffins
Broccoli Cornbread
Pumpkin Apple Muffins
Easy Biscuits
Southern Corn Sticks
Squash Dressing
Blueberry Tea Loaf

"Jesus said to them,
'I am the bread of life;
he who comes to Me shall not hunger,
and he who believes in Me
shall never thirst'."

John 6:35

PUMPKIN BREAD

3½ cups all purpose flour	1 cup oil
2 teaspoons soda	4 eggs
1½ teaspoons salt	⅔ cup water
1 teaspoon cinnamon	1 cup pumpkin
1 teaspoon nutmeg	1 cup chopped nuts
3 cups sugar	

- Sift flour and next 5 ingredients into a mixing bowl. Blend well. Add oil, eggs, water, and pumpkin. Mix until smooth. Stir in nuts.

- Pour into 2 greased loaf pans.

- Bake at 350° for 1 hour.

    Yield: 2 loaves

Ginny Cole

STRAWBERRY BREAD

4 eggs	3 cups flour
2 packages strawberries, frozen	1 teaspoon salt
1 cup oil	1 teaspoon baking soda
1 cup chopped pecans	1 tablespoon cinnamon

- Combine eggs, strawberries, and oil. Fold in pecans. Set aside.

- Combine remaining ingredients. Add to egg mixture, blending well.

- Pour batter into 2 greased 9x5x3-inch loaf pans.

- Bake at 350° for 60 to 70 minutes.

    Yield: 2 loaves

Aimee Nelson

CARROT LOAF

2 cups sugar
3 cups flour
1 teaspoon soda
½ teaspoon salt
1 teaspoon cinnamon
2 cups grated carrot
1⅓ cups oil

2 eggs, beaten
1 cup chopped nuts
1 cup crushed pineapple
1 teaspoon vanilla
1 teaspoon lemon extract
1 teaspoon almond extract

- Combine sugar with next 4 ingredients in a large bowl. Add carrots, oil, and eggs beating until well mixed. Add nuts and next 4 ingredients, mixing well.

- Pour batter into two 8x5-inch loaf pans or 3 small loaf pans which have been greased and floured.

- Bake at 350° for 1 hour.

Yield: 2 loaves

This is delicious as either bread or cake.

Linda Dennis

SOUR CREAM MUFFINS

½ cup butter, melted
1 cup sour cream

1 cup self-rising flour

- Mix butter and sour cream; add flour.

- Spoon into mini-muffin tins.

- Bake at 350° until lightly browned.

Yield: 1 dozen

Gale Belser

ZUCCHINI BREAD

3 eggs	1 teaspoon salt
2 cups sugar	½ teaspoon baking powder
1 cup oil	1½ cups flour
2 cups unpeeled zucchini, grated	1½ cups whole wheat flour
1 tablespoon vanilla	1 cup chopped pecans
1½ tablespoons cinnamon	1 cup raisins
2 teaspoons soda	

- Beat eggs until light and foamy. Add sugar and oil, beating well. Stir in zucchini and vanilla.
- Mix cinnamon and next 7 ingredients. Add to zucchini mixture and mix well.
- Pour batter into 2 greased loaf pans.
- Bake at 350s for 50 minutes.

  Yield: 2 loaves

Cindy Kapp

LEMON-RASPBERRY MUFFINS

2 cups self-rising flour	1 teaspoon lemon extract
1 cup sugar	2 eggs
1 cup half-and-half	1 cup fresh or frozen raspberries,
½ cup oil	without syrup (do not thaw)

- Combine flour and sugar in a large bowl.
- Mix half-and-half, oil, lemon extract, and eggs in a small bowl and blend well.
- Add egg mixture to dry ingredients. Stir until moistened. Fold in raspberries.
- Spoon batter into greased muffin tins, filling cups ¾ full.
- Bake at 425° for 18 to 23 minutes. Cool for 5 minutes; remove from pan.

  Yield: 12 to 16 muffins

Bo Lachicotte

BRAN MUFFINS

2 cups boiling water	5 cups flour
6 cups all bran cereal, divided	5 teaspoons baking soda
1 cup canola oil	2 teaspoons salt
4 eggs, beaten	28 ounces apple butter
3 cups dark brown sugar, packed	2 cups chopped walnuts
1 quart buttermilk	1 cup raisins

- Pour boiling water over 2 cups of bran. Add oil. Mix and set aside.

- Mix together eggs, sugar, buttermilk, and the remaining bran in that order.

- Sift flour with soda and salt. Combine bran mixtures with flour mixture. Stir in apple butter, walnuts, and raisins.

- Spoon batter into greased muffin tins.

- Bake at 400° for 15 to 20 minutes.

Yield: 6 dozen

Mixture keeps 6 weeks in refrigerator. Muffins freeze well.

Barbara Hood

SALLIE'S BISCUITS

2 cups self-rising flour	½ cup shortening
½ teaspoon sugar	1 cup buttermilk

- Blend flour with sugar. Cut in shortening with pastry knife. Stir in buttermilk.

- Place soft dough from bowl onto well-floured surface and knead lightly. Flatten with hands to about 1½ inches.

- Cut with well-floured juice glass. Prick each biscuit with a fork.

- Bake at 450° for 10 to 15 minutes or until golden brown.

Yield: 20 biscuits

May bake and freeze.

Aimee Nelson

BLUEBERRY MUFFINS

½ cup butter
1 cup sugar
2 eggs
2 cups flour
2 teaspoons baking powder

½ teaspoon salt
½ cup milk
1 teaspoon vanilla
2½ cups blueberries, divided

- Cream butter and sugar in a large bowl until smooth. Add eggs, one at a time, beating well after each addition. Set aside.

- Combine flour, baking powder, and salt; add alternately to the creamed mixture with the milk and vanilla that have been mixed together.

- Crush ½ cup blueberries; add to batter. Fold in remaining blueberries. Spoon batter into greased muffin tins, filling cups ⅔ full.

- Bake at 375° for 30 minutes. Cool in pan for 5 minutes; remove from pan.

Yield: 12 to 18 muffins

Aimee Nelson

BROCCOLI CORNBREAD

1 (10-ounce) box frozen chopped
  broccoli, thawed and drained
1 box cornbread mix
¼ cup margarine, melted
2 tablespoons mayonnaise

1 small onion, chopped
2 eggs, beaten
½ cup cottage cheese
¾ teaspoon salt

- Mix all ingredients together well. Spoon in a greased 13x9x2-inch pan.

- Bake at 350° for 30 to 35 minutes.

Yield: 15 servings

This freezes well after baking. Just reheat and serve.

Aimee Kornegay
Muff Lyons

May substitute 2 cups chopped squash for broccoli.

Frances Leitner

PUMPKIN APPLE MUFFINS

2½ cups flour
2 cups sugar
1 tablespoon pumpkin spice
1 teaspoon baking soda
½ teaspoon salt

2 eggs, lightly beaten
1 cup solid packed pumpkin
½ cup vegetable oil
2 cups finely chopped apples

- Combine flour with next 4 ingredients; set aside.
- Mix eggs, pumpkin, and oil in a medium bowl.
- Add egg mixture to dry ingredients. Stir until moistened. Stir in apples. Spoon batter into greased muffin tins, filling tins ⅔ full.
- Prepare streusel topping. Sprinkle topping on muffins.
- Bake at 350° for 35 to 40 minutes or until toothpick inserted in center comes out clean.

STREUSEL TOPPING

2 tablespoons flour
¼ cup sugar

½ teaspoon cinnamon
4 teaspoons butter

- Mix flour, sugar, and cinnamon. Cut in butter with a fork.
  Yield: 18 muffins

  For 6 large muffins increase baking time to 40 to 45 minutes.

  Beth Barker

EASY BISCUITS

2 cups self-rising flour

1 cup heavy cream or
1 cup sour cream

- Combine flour and cream.
- Roll or pat out dough, on lightly floured surface, to ¼-inch thick. Cut with small biscuit cutter. Place on a lightly greased baking sheet.
- Bake at 425° for 10 to 12 minutes.
  Yield: 12 biscuits

  Mary Alice Beck
  Tag Wylie

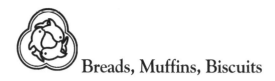

SOUTHERN CORN STICKS

½ cup yellow corn meal
½ cup flour
1 tablespoon sugar
2 teaspoons baking powder

¼ teaspoon salt
1 egg, beaten
½ cup evaporated skim milk
2 tablespoons vegetable oil

- Combine corn meal with next 4 ingredients. Stir well and set aside.

- Combine egg, milk, and oil. Add egg mixture to dry ingredients, stirring until just smooth.

- Coat a cast-iron cornstick pan with cooking spray. Heat pan in a 425° oven for 3 minutes or until hot. Remove pan from oven. Spoon batter into pan, filling ⅔ full.

- Bake at 425° for 10 to 12 minutes or until lightly browned.

Yield: 1 dozen cornsticks

Aimee Kornegay

May add 1 tablespoon finely chopped red bell pepper, 1 tablespoon minced jalapeño pepper and ⅛ teaspoon garlic powder to above ingredients; omit sugar.

SQUASH DRESSING

1 small onion, chopped
½ cup margarine
2 eggs, beaten
2 cups squash, cooked, drained
and mashed

1 can cream of chicken soup
1 package Mexican cornbread mix
black pepper to taste

- Sauté onion in margarine until tender.

- Combine remaining ingredients, mixing well.

- Pour batter into a greased 8 x 8 x 2-inch casserole.

- Bake at 350° for 25 minutes.

Yield: 6 to 8 servings

BLUEBERRY TEA LOAF

2½ cups flour
2 teaspoons baking powder
¼ teaspoon nutmeg
¼ teaspoon salt
½ cup butter, softened

1 cup sugar
2 eggs
1 cup milk
1 cup blueberries (if frozen, thaw
   and drain)

- Sift flour with baking powder, nutmeg, and salt. Set aside. In a large bowl, with electric mixer at high speed, beat butter with sugar and eggs until light and fluffy, about 2 minutes. At low speed, stir in flour mixture (in fourths) alternately with milk (in thirds), beginning and ending flour mixture. Mix just until smooth.

- Fold in blueberries gently. Pour into a greased 9x5x2¾-inch loaf pan.

- Bake at 350° for 60 to 65 minutes or until cake tester inserted in center comes out clean.

- Cool in pan or wire rack for 20 minutes. Turn out of pan onto wire rack; sprinkle with powdered sugar. Serve warm or cold.

Yield: 1 loaf

A wonderful way to use our delicious local blueberries.

Tecla Earnshaw

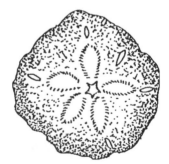

SWEETS

CAKES

Friendship Cake
Apple Cake
Orange Slice Cake
Best Cheesecake
My Grandmother's Fudge Cupcakes
Elegant Buttermilk Pound Cake
Butternut Pound Cake
Chocolate Pound Cake
Frosting for Chocolate Pound Cake
Cold Oven Pound Cake
Caramel Frosting
Walnut Pound Cake
Cream Icing for Pound Cake
Sour Cream Pound Cake
Heavenly Chocolate Nut Cake
"Island" Rum Cake
V.V.'s Very, Very Sherry Cake

PIES

Peach Goody
Old Fashioned Apple Pie
Blueberry Cream Pie
Apple Crisp a la Mode
Tennessee Cobbler
Gertrude's Original
∝   Blackberry Crisp
Cranberry Apple Bake
Pecan Chocolate Chip Pie
Pecan Pie
"Chart House" Mud Pie
Chocolate Chess Pie
Lemon Chess Pie
Peanut Butter Pie
Raisin Cream Pie

DESSERTS

Lemon Lush
Praline Sauce
Four Layer Cake
∝ Chocolate Eclair Squares
Bobo's Chocolate Roll

Pumpkin Roll
Creamy Banana Pudding
"No-Cook" Banana Pudding
Lemon Curd
Pastry Shells
Angel Bavarian Cake
∝ Pot de Crème
Tiramisu
Eggnog Cake
Old Fashioned Boiled Custard
Charlotte Russe
Grand Marnier Sauce
David's Chocolate Pecan Mousse
     with Sabayon Sauce
"Ole Timey" Gingerbread
     with Lemon Sauce
Baked Flan with Caramel
Perfect Peach Ice Cream

COOKIES

Praline Grahams
Edisto Pecan Dream Bars
Male Cakes
Gooey Bars
Oatmeal Cookies
Brownies Savannah Style
Easy Oatmeal Cookies
Snickerdoodles
Toffee Bars
Double Gingersnaps
Toffee Squares
Strawberry Cookies
Caramel Squares
Raspberry Squares

CANDIES

Candied Violets
Mock Heath Bars
Never Fail Fudge
Pralines
English Toffee

"Pleasant words are a honeycomb,
sweet to the soul and healing to the bones."
Proverbs 16:24

FRIENDSHIP CAKE

1 cup greetings	⅔ cup love
½ cup smiles	1 tablespoon sympathy
1 large handshake	2 cups hospitality

- Cream greetings and smiles thoroughly; add handshake separately and stir in love slowly.

- Sift sympathy and hospitality and fold in carefully.

- Bake in a warm heart.

- Serve often.

Aimee Reese

APPLE CAKE

3 cups flour	1¼ cups oil
1½ teaspoons baking soda	2 teaspoons vanilla
½ teaspoon salt	4 cups chopped apples (Granny
1 teaspoon cinnamon	Smith or Golden Delicious)
2 eggs	1 cup chopped pecans
1¾ cups sugar	1 cup raisins (optional)
½ cup brown sugar	

- Sift together flour, soda, salt, and cinnamon. Set aside.

- Beat eggs and sugars until creamy; add oil and vanilla, beating until smooth.

- Add dry ingredients and mix until a stiff dough forms; stir in apples and pecans.

- Pour batter into a greased and floured 10-inch tube pan, 13x9x2-inch pan or 2 loaf pans.

- Bake at 350° for 1 hour or until done.

  Yield: 1 cake

Bo Lachicotte, Veda Godwin

May substitute pears for apples.

ORANGE SLICE CAKE

1 cup butter
1 box powdered sugar
6 eggs
4½ cups sifted cake flour,
   reserving ½ cup to coat
   fruit and nuts

2 teaspoons vanilla
1½ cups chopped dates
1½ cups chopped nuts
1½ cups chopped candied
   orange slices
½ cup flaked coconut

- Cream butter and sugar; add eggs, one at a time, beating after each addition.

- Add flour and vanilla, gradually, beating constantly. Fold in fruit and nuts, which have been coated with flour.

- Pour into a greased and floured 10-inch tube pan or 2 loaf pans.

- Bake at 300° for 1½ hours.

- Prepare glaze. Puncture cake with ice pick while hot and pour glaze over cake, spooning over several times.

GLAZE

2 cups powdered sugar
1 cup orange juice

1 tablespoon grated orange zest

- Combine ingredients and mix until sugar dissolves.

Yield: 1 cake

Annabelle Creech

BEST CHEESECAKE

So-o-o good and creamy!

2 (8-ounce) packages cream cheese
4 egg yolks
1 teaspoon lemon juice
¾ cup sugar

1 teaspoon vanilla
4 egg whites, stiffly beaten
graham cracker crust

- Combine cream cheese and next 4 ingredients; beat with an electric mixer for 10 to 15 minutes. Fold in egg whites and pour into crust.

- Bake at 350° for 30 minutes.

- Prepare topping. Spread on cooled cake.

- Bake at 350° for 5 minutes.

TOPPING

1 cup sour cream
2 tablespoons sugar

½ teaspoon vanilla

- Combine sour cream, sugar, and vanilla and mix well.

Yield: 12 servings

Linda Dennis

MY GRANDMOTHER'S FUDGE CUPCAKES

1¾ cups sugar
1 cup flour
4 eggs
4 ounces semi-sweet chocolate

1 cup butter
1½ cups chopped pecans
1 teaspoon vanilla

- Combine sugar, flour, and eggs; blend well but do not beat. Set aside.

- Melt chocolate and margarine in a saucepan; add nuts and stir; add vanilla and blend. Do not beat. Pour into flour mixture and blend well.

- Spoon into paper lined muffin tins.

- Bake at 350° for 30 minutes.

Yield: 2 dozen cupcakes

Courtney Tutas, Gale Belser

ELEGANT BUTTERMILK POUND CAKE

This cake is one of the very best!

½ cup butter, softened	½ teaspoon salt
½ cup shortening	1 tablespoon boiling water
3 cups sugar	½ teaspoon baking soda
5 eggs	1 cup buttermilk
3 cups flour	2 teaspoons vanilla

- Cream butter, shortening, and sugar; add eggs and beat well.

- Combine flour and salt; dissolve soda in boiling water and add to buttermilk.

- Add dry ingredients and buttermilk, alternately to creamed mixture; beat well; blend in vanilla and pour into a greased and floured tube pan.

- Bake at 300° for 1½ hours or until done.

Yield: 1 cake

Van Leer Rowe

BUTTERNUT POUND CAKE

"Miss Earnestine" was a friend to everyone on the Island and cooked for many. This pound cake was enjoyed by all.

1 cup butter, softened	3 cups flour
½ cup shortening	1 teaspoon baking powder
3 cups sugar	1 cup milk
5 eggs	1 teaspoon butternut flavoring

- Cream butter, shortening, and sugar. Add eggs, one at a time, blending well after each addition.

- Add flour and baking powder alternately with milk; add flavoring.

- Pour batter into a greased and floured 10-inch tube pan.

- Bake, do not preheat, at 325° for 1½ hours.

Yield: 1 cake

Barbara Hood, Earnestine Burnell

CHOCOLATE POUND CAKE

This is a chocolate lover's treat.

1 cup butter, softened
½ cup shortening
3 cups sugar
5 eggs
3 cups flour, sifted
½ teaspoon baking powder

½ teaspoon salt
4 to 8 tablespoons cocoa
1 cup milk
1 tablespoon vanilla
powdered sugar

- Cream butter, shortening, and sugar; add eggs, one at a time, beating until smooth.

- Combine flour, baking powder, salt, and cocoa. Add dry ingredients to creamed mixture alternately with milk; blend well and add vanilla.

- Pour into a greased and floured 10-inch tube or bundt pan.

- Bake at 325° for 1 hour and 20 minutes.

- Cool 30 minutes on a rack, loosen sides with a knife and turn out; sprinkle with powdered sugar if desired.

  Yield: 1 cake

  Randolph Berretta, Aimee Nelson

FROSTING FOR CHOCOLATE POUND CAKE

¼ cup butter or margarine,
  softened
2 teaspoons vanilla

1 box powdered sugar
½ cup cocoa
milk

- Combine all ingredients with enough milk to form spreading consistency.

- Add cream and beat well.

- Add powdered sugar and vanilla.

- Beat until icing reaches desired consistency.

  Aimee Nelson

COLD OVEN POUND CAKE

1 cup butter or margarine	3 cups flour
½ cup shortening	½ teaspoon salt
3 cups sugar	1 cup milk
5 eggs	1 tablespoon vanilla

- Cream butter and shortening; add sugar and beat with electric mixer for 10 minutes or until almost white. Add eggs, one at a time, blending well after each addition.

- Sift flour and salt together, after measuring. Add to egg mixture alternately with milk, blending well.

- Pour into a greased and floured 10-inch tube pan.

- Start in cold oven; when temperature reaches 300° bake for 1½ hours or until cake leaves sides of pan. Cool 20 minutes; turn out.

  Yield: 1 cake

Aimee Reese

CARAMEL FROSTING

The Thursday Morning Bridge Club's most requested.

¼ cup butter, melted	¼ cup milk
1 cup brown sugar, firmly packed	2 cups powdered sugar, sifted

- Combine butter and brown sugar in a saucepan; boil over low heat for 2 minutes stirring constantly.

- Add milk; continue stirring until mixture comes to a boil. Remove from heat and cool.

- Add powdered sugar and beat until smooth. Spread on cake of choice.

  May be doubled.

Elva Richards

WALNUT POUND CAKE

This cake has been enjoyed by family and friends for years.

1 cup butter
2 tablespoons vegetable shortening
3 cups sugar
5 eggs
3 cups cake flour

½ pint heavy cream
1¼ teaspoons vanilla
1 cup chopped walnuts
dry sherry (optional)

- Cream butter, shortening, and sugar until smooth. Add eggs, one at a time, stirring well after each addition.

- Add flour and blend well. Stir in cream, vanilla, and nuts.

- Pour batter into a greased and floured tube or bundt pan.

- Start in cold oven; when temperature reaches 300°, bake for 1½ hours or until done. Pour sherry over warm cake.

- Cool cake in pan for 10 minutes. Remove.

  Yield: 1 cake

Judy Inman

CREAM ICING FOR POUND CAKE

1 (8-ounce) package cream cheese
½ cup butter or margarine
1 box powdered sugar

1 tablespoon vanilla
1 cup chopped pecans (optional)

- Cream butter and cream cheese.

- Add sugar and vanilla and cream well. Spread on cool cake.

Aimee Nelson

SOUR CREAM POUND CAKE

1 cup butter, softened
3 cups sugar
6 eggs
3 cups flour
¼ teaspoon baking soda

¼ teaspoon salt
1 cup sour cream
1 teaspoon vanilla
1 teaspoon almond extract

- Cream butter and sugar until smooth; add eggs, one at a time, beating just until yellow disappears.

- Combine flour, soda, and salt.

- Add dry ingredients and sour cream, alternately, to creamed mixture, beginning and ending with flour mixture. Stir in flavorings.

- Spoon batter into a greased and floured 10-inch tube pan.

- Bake at 325° for 1½ hours or until done.

Yield: 1 cake

Barbara Hood

1½ cups butter, 1 tablespoon lemon juice, ¾ teaspoon vanilla, cake flour. No salt, baking soda, or almond extract.

LePage Bailey

HEAVENLY CHOCOLATE NUT CAKE

This is the best! Your friends will ask for the recipe.

1 cup butter, softened	2 eggs
2 cups sugar	1½ cups milk
1⅓ cups chocolate chips, melted	2¼ teaspoons vanilla
2 cups self-rising flour, sifted	1¼ cups chopped pecans

- Cream butter and sugar. Add chocolate, blend, and add flour.

- Add eggs alternately with milk. Beat well after each addition. Stir in vanilla and pecans. Pour into a greased bundt or tube pan.

- Bake at 350° for 1 hour. Cool 10 minutes in pan. Remove.

- Prepare icing. Spread on cooled cake.

Icing

½ cup butter	1¼ teaspoons vanilla
⅔ cup chocolate chips	1 teaspoon lemon juice
1 egg white	1 cup chopped pecans
1½ cups powdered sugar	

- Melt butter and chips; add egg white and beat lightly. Add remaining ingredients and beat to spreading consistency.

Yield: 1 cake

Van Leer Rowe

"ISLAND" RUM CAKE

Irresistably good!

1 cup nut meats, chopped,
   reserve ¼ cup
1 package yellow cake mix
1 small package instant
   vanilla pudding

4 eggs
½ cup vegetable oil
½ cup water
½ cup rum

- Grease and flour a bundt cake pan. Sprinkle with reserved nut meats.

- Combine remaining ingredients; mix well and pour into pan.

- Bake at 325° for 50 to 60 minutes.

- Prepare glaze. Pour over hot cake, pulling cake away from sides of pan; cool ½ hour before removing cake from pan.

GLAZE

¼ cup rum
¼ cup water

½ cup margarine
1 cup sugar

- Combine ingredients in a saucepan and boil 2 minutes.

Yield: 1 cake

Frances Leitner

V. V.'S VERY, VERY SHERRY CAKE

This always receives a compliment.

1 package yellow cake mix
1 large package instant
   vanilla pudding
4 eggs, beaten

¾ cup oil
¾ cup cream sherry
1 teaspoon nutmeg (optional)

- Combine all ingredients; beat at medium speed for 5 minutes.

- Pour into a greased and floured 10-inch tube or bundt pan.

- Bake at 350° for 45 minutes.

- Cool 10 minutes in pan. Remove from pan; prick top of cake with a toothpick.

- Prepare glaze; drizzle on warm cake.

GLAZE

¼ cup cream sherry

1 cup powdered sugar

- Combine sherry and sugar; mix well.

Yield: 1 cake

Keeps well. May be made 1 or 2 days ahead.

V. V. Thompson

PEACH GOODIE

Easy and wonderful!

1 quart sliced peaches or more
½ cup margarine, melted

1 cup self-rising flour
1 cup sugar

- Place peaches into a 2-quart casserole dish.

- Combine remaining ingredients; mix well and pour over fruit.

- Bake at 350° for 30 to 40 minutes.

Yield: 6 to 8 servings

Kat Hunt

233

OLD FASHIONED APPLE PIE

Everyone loves this!

1 cup sugar
1½ tablespoons flour
¼ teaspoon nutmeg
½ teaspoon cinnamon
6 large Granny Smith apples,
   peeled, and thinly sliced

2 tablespoons butter
2 tablespoons lemon juice
2 (9-inch) refrigerated pastry
   shells, unbaked

- Line pie plate with 1 pastry shell.

- Combine sugar, flour, nutmeg, and cinnamon; mix well.

- Toss apples with mixture and place in pastry. Dot with butter and sprinkle with lemon juice. Cover with remaining pastry, seal edges, and slit top several times.

- Bake at 350° for 1 hour. Serve plain or with cheese or ice cream.

Yield: 6 to 8 servings

A few spoonfuls of mincemeat may be added with apples for variety.

Cindy Kapp

BLUEBERRY CREAM PIE

So easy! A wonderful summertime dessert!

1 (12-ounce) carton frozen
   whipped topping, thawed
1 can sweetened condensed milk
4 tablespoons lemon juice

4 cups fresh blueberries
2 (9-inch) graham cracker pie
   crusts, baked and cooled

- Fold together (do not beat) topping, milk, lemon juice, and berries. Pour into crusts.

- Refrigerate or freeze until firm.

Yield: 6 to 8 servings

Walton Salley

APPLE CRISP A LA MODE

So-o-o yummy

8 apples, peeled and diced
¼ cup water
1 cup flour
1½ cups uncooked oatmeal

¾ cup brown sugar
1 teaspoon cinnamon
½ cup margarine, softened
1 quart low fat frozen yogurt

- Place apples and water into an 8x8x2-inch baking dish.

- Combine flour, oatmeal, sugar, and cinnamon. Add margarine; blend until crumbly. Spread over apples.

- Bake at 350° for 45 minutes. Serve warm with yogurt.

Yield: 8 servings

Bo Lachicotte

Substitute peaches for apples; add one cup chopped pecans. Top with ice cream.

Veda Godwin

TENNESSEE COBBLER

½ cup butter
1 cup sugar
1 cup self-rising flour

1 cup milk
4 cups sliced fresh peaches
  or blueberries

- Melt butter in a 1½-quart round glass baking dish.

- Combine sugar, flour, and milk and pour over butter. Do not stir.

- Place fruit on top of batter.

- Bake at 350° for 45 minutes. Serve with topping of whipped cream or ice cream.

Yield: 6 to 8 servings

Ellie Howard, Brenda Lewis

GERTRUDE'S ORIGINAL BLACKBERRY CRISP

4 cups blackberries
1¼ cups sugar, divided
½ cup water
1 teaspoon vanilla
1 cup flour

1 teaspoon baking powder
½ teaspoon salt
1 egg, lightly beaten
⅓ cup margarine, melted and
  cooled

- Combine blackberries, ½ cup sugar, water, and vanilla and place in an 8x8x2-inch baking dish.

- Combine flour, baking powder, salt, and ¾ cup sugar; add egg and mix until crumbly. Sprinkle on berry mixture and drizzle with margarine.

- Bake at 350° for 35 minutes. Serve warm or cold.

Yield: 6 to 8 servings

Gertrude Woods

CRANBERRY APPLE BAKE

This is really good and so appropriate for Thanksgiving.

3 cups apples, unpeeled and cut
  into bite-sized pieces
2 cups raw cranberries

¾ to 1½ cups sugar, according to
  sweetness of apples

- Mix apples, cranberries, and sugar in a 13x9x2-inch glass casserole dish.

- Prepare nut topping and spread on top of apple mixture and dot with butter.

- Bake at 350° for 1 hour.

NUT TOPPING

1½ cups oatmeal
⅓ cup flour
½ cup brown sugar

1 cup chopped pecans
½ cup butter

- Mix oatmeal, flour, sugar, and pecans.

Yield: 6 to 8 servings

Debbie Brockman

PECAN CHOCOLATE CHIP PIE

Great when warm with a scoop of ice cream on top.

1 cup sugar
1 cup light corn syrup
4 eggs
½ cup butter, melted

1 teaspoon vanilla
6 ounces chocolate chips
1 cup chopped pecans
2 (9-inch) pie shells, unbaked

- Combine sugar, syrup, and eggs and mix well. Add butter, vanilla, chips, and pecans and stir well. Pour into pastry shells.

- Bake at 350° for 40 minutes or until set.

  Yield: 12 to 16 servings

  Freezes well.

V.V. Thompson

PECAN PIE

1 cup broken pecans
1 (9-inch) pie shell, unbaked
½ cup butter or margarine, melted
3 eggs, beaten
¼ cup sugar

1 cup light brown sugar
1 cup light corn syrup
1 teaspoon vanilla
pinch of salt

- Sprinkle pecans on bottom of pie shell.

- Mix eggs and remaining ingredients. Pour into pie shell.

- Bake at 325° for one hour.

  Yield: 6 to 8 servings

  Add 1 more cup of broken pecans to recipe and it will make 2 pies. This freezes well.

Josita Montgomery

"CHART HOUSE" MUD PIE

½ package chocolate wafers, crushed
¼ cup butter, melted

1 quart coffee ice cream, softened
1½ cups fudge sauce, cold

- Combine wafers and butter; mix well. Press into a 9-inch pie pan; cover with ice cream.
- Freeze until ice cream is firm; top with fudge sauce.
- Return to freezer for 10 hours or overnight.
- Serve with a dollop of whipped cream and sliced almonds.

  Yield: 6 to 8 servings

CHOCOLATE CHESS PIE

A big hit!

½ cup butter, melted
2 squares unsweetened
   chocolate, melted
1 cup sugar

2 eggs, beaten
pinch of salt
1 teaspoon vanilla
1 (9-inch) pie shell, unbaked

- Combine first 6 ingredients and pour into pie shell.
- Bake at 350° for 35 minutes.

  Yield: 6 to 8 servings

  May top with whipped cream or vanilla ice cream.

Catherine Arnot

LEMON CHESS PIE

Easy and good.

2 cups sugar
4 eggs, lightly beaten
½ cup butter, softened
2 tablespoons cornstarch

½ cup lemon juice
¼ cup lemon zest
2 (9-inch) pie shells, unbaked

- Combine sugar and next 5 ingredients; mix well. Pour into pie shells.
- Bake at 350° for 45 minutes. Serve with a dollop of whipped cream.

Yield: 12 to 16 servings

Instead of cornstarch, 1 tablespoon cornmeal and 1 tablespoon flour may be substituted.

Aimee Nelson

PEANUT BUTTER PIE

Easy, light, and wonderful!

1 (9-inch) pie shell, baked
¾ cup powdered sugar
⅓ cup chunky peanut butter

1 small package vanilla pudding,
    prepared (not instant)
frozen whipped topping

- Blend sugar and peanut butter with pastry blender; mixture will be crumbly.
- Pour onto bottom of pie shell, reserving ¼ cup for top of pie.
- Pour pudding over first mixture; cover with topping and sprinkle with reserved crumbs.
- Chill until ready to serve.

Yield: 6 to 8 servings

Joan Foxworth

RAISIN CREAM PIE

This pie has a smooth butterscotch taste.

1 (9-inch) pie shell, baked
   and cooled
1 cup raisins
1 cup sugar

1 (12-ounce) can evaporated milk
4½ tablespoons cornstarch
2 egg yolks, beaten

- Cover raisins with cold water; boil until tender (10 to 15 minutes), drain and put into top of a double boiler.

- Add sugar, milk, and cornstarch; cook until thickened. Add yolks and continue cooking until well blended. Pour into pie shell.

- Prepare meringue. Spread over filling sealing to edge of pastry.

- Bake at 375° until brown.

MERINGUE

2 egg whites
¼ teaspoon cream of tartar

2 tablespoons sugar
⅛ teaspoon salt

- Beat egg whites and cream of tartar until soft peaks form; gradually add sugar and salt and beat until stiff peaks form.

Yield: 6 to 8 servings

Gwen Hughes

LEMON LUSH

A wonderful summertime dessert!

1 cup flour
1 tablespoon sugar
½ cup margarine, softened
1 cup chopped nuts
1 (8-ounce) package cream cheese
1 cup powdered sugar

1 (16-ounce) carton frozen
  whipped topping, divided
2 small packages instant
  lemon pudding
2½ cups cold milk

- Layer 1: Combine flour, sugar, and margarine with hands. Add nuts and spread in a greased 13x9x2-inch baking dish. Bake at 350° for 15 to 20 minutes until golden brown.

- Layer 2: Blend cream cheese, powdered sugar, and 1 cup topping in mixer until smooth. Spread over first layer (crust).

- Layer 3: Blend pudding and milk and spread over second layer (cheese).

- Layer 4: Spread remaining topping on top of third layer (pudding). Sprinkle with chopped nuts. Chill for at least 2 hours or overnight. Cut into squares and serve.

Yield: 15 servings

Gale Belser

PRALINE SAUCE

1½ cups light brown sugar
⅔ cup light corn syrup
¼ cup butter

1 small can evaporated milk
pecans

- Combine sugar, syrup, and butter. Bring to a boil. Remove from heat and cool to lukewarm. Add milk and blend well.

- Store in a jar in refrigerator. Serve over ice cream with pecans sprinkled on top.

Yield: 3½ cups

Keeps for a long time. Can be re-heated over and over again.

Aimee Kornegay

241

'Pon Top Edisto

FOUR LAYER CAKE

A chocolate lover's delight!

½ cup margarine
1 cup flour
1 cup pecans, chopped
1 (8-ounce) package cream cheese
1 cup powdered sugar

1 (16-ounce) carton frozen
  whipped topping
2 small boxes instant chocolate
  pudding mix
3 cups milk
1 package slivered almonds, toasted

- Layer 1: Mix margarine, flour, and pecans. Spread evenly on bottom of 13x9x2-inch baking dish. Cook at 350° for 10 minutes.

- Layer 2: Mix cheese and sugar until smooth. Fold in 1 cup topping. Put on first layer before it cools completely.

- Layer 3: Add milk to chocolate pudding mix. Mix for 2 minutes. Let stand for 2 minutes. Place on top of second layer.

- Layer 4: Spread remaining topping over third layer. Top with toasted almonds. Chill at least 6 hours or overnight. Cut in squares and serve.

Yield: 15 servings

Gale Belser

CHOCOLATE ECLAIR SQUARES ⊂×

1 pound box graham crackers
2 small packages instant French
  vanilla pudding

3 cups milk
1 (12-ounce) container non-dairy
  whipped topping

- Line a greased 13x9x2-inch glass dish with whole graham crackers.

- Prepare pudding, using 3 cups milk according to package directions; fold in whipped topping.

- Spread half of pudding mixture over graham crackers; repeat cracker and pudding mixture layers. Top with a layer of crackers.

- Prepare icing. Ice pie and refrigerate overnight.

ICING

3 ounces semi-sweet chocolate chips
2 teaspoons light corn syrup
3 tablespoons butter

1 teaspoon vanilla
1½ cups sifted powdered sugar
3 tablespoons milk

- Melt chips, syrup, and butter. Stir in vanilla, sugar, and milk.

Yield: 15 servings

Veda Godwin, Judie Nye, Jean Reid

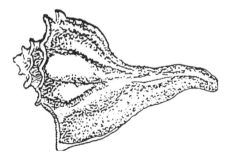

BOBO'S CHOCOLATE ROLL

Sinfully delicious!

7 eggs, separated	7 tablespoons sugar, heaping
7 tablespoons cocoa	1 pint heavy cream

- Whip egg yolks until frothy; add cocoa and sugar and beat until well blended. Whip egg whites until stiff but not dry; fold into chocolate mixture. Spread into a greased and floured jelly-roll pan.

- Bake at 325° for 18 minutes.

- Moisten a kitchen towel; invert pan onto towel; roll up cake in towel. Allow to cool.

- Beat cream until thick; carefully unroll cake and spread with cream. Reroll.

- Prepare icing. Spread on sides and ends of roll; allow to set up. Lift and ice bottom.

ICING

1 box powdered sugar	¼ cup butter, melted
4 tablespoons cocoa, heaping	1 teaspoon vanilla

- Combine first three ingredients, adding boiling water until mixture reaches spreading consistency. Stir until smooth and add vanilla. If too runny, add more sugar.

Yield: 10 servings

Robert E. "Bobo" Lee, The Pavilion Restaurant

PUMPKIN ROLL

Makes a very good and pretty dessert.

3 eggs
1 cup sugar
⅔ cup cooked pumpkin, mashed
1 teaspoon lemon juice
¾ cup flour
2 teaspoons ground cinnamon

1 teaspoon baking powder
½ teaspoon salt
1 teaspoon ground ginger
1 teaspoon ground nutmeg
¼ cup powdered sugar

- Beat eggs for 5 minutes at high speed of electric mixer. Add sugar gradually, beating well. Stir in pumpkin and lemon juice.

- Combine flour and next 5 ingredients. Add to pumpkin mixture and blend well. Spoon batter into a greased and floured 15x10x1-inch jelly-roll pan, spreading evenly to corners.

- Bake at 375° for 15 minutes. Turn cake onto a towel. Sprinkle with ¼ cup powdered sugar. Begin at narrow end; roll cake and towel together, jelly-roll fashion; cool.

- Prepare filling. Unroll cake and spread with filling. Roll cake up again and chill, seam side down.

FILLING

1 cup powdered sugar
1 (8-ounce) package cream
cheese, softened

¼ cup butter
½ teaspoon vanilla

- Combine all ingredients and beat until smooth and creamy.

Yield: 10 servings

Annabelle Creech

245

CREAMY BANANA PUDDING

A very rich banana pudding.

1 (14-ounce) can sweetened
   condensed milk
1½ cups cold water
1 small package instant vanilla
   pudding mix

1 pint heavy cream, whipped
1 box vanilla wafers
4-5 bananas, sliced

• Combine condensed milk and water in a large bowl. Add pudding mix and beat well. Chill 5 minutes. Fold in whipped cream.

• Spoon 1 cup pudding mixture into a 2½-quart glass serving bowl. Top with ⅓ each of the wafers, bananas, and pudding. Repeat layers twice, ending with pudding.

• Chill thoroughly before serving.

Yield: 8 to 10 servings

Van Leer Rowe

"NO COOK" BANANA PUDDING

1 large package instant vanilla
   pudding, prepared
1 (8-ounce) carton sour cream
1 teaspoon vanilla

4-5 bananas, sliced
1 box vanilla wafers
1 (8-ounce) carton frozen
   whipped topping

• Add sour cream and vanilla to prepared pudding. Mix well.

• Layer, in a 3-quart bowl, wafers, bananas, and pudding. Repeat layers and cover with topping. Refrigerate.

Yield: 6 to 8 servings

Sallie Fontaine

LEMON CURD

This recipe comes from Sweden and it never fails to charm guests.

2 eggs
2 egg yolks
2 lemons, juice and zest

½ cup butter
½ cup to 1 cup sugar

- Put eggs and yolks into the top of a double boiler. Beat gently until mixed.

- Add juice, zest, butter, and sugar. Cook over hot water stirring constantly with a wooden spoon until thickened. Chill.

- Serve in tart shells topped with unsweetened whipped cream.

Yield: 1½ pints

Will keep one month in refrigerator in a tightly closed jar. Good on hot biscuits or fresh fruit.

Aimee Kornegay, Frances Richardson

PASTRY SHELLS

1 cup plus 2 tablespoons flour
2 tablespoons Parmesan cheese
½ cup butter

1 egg, beaten
¼ teaspoon salt

- Mix flour and remaining ingredients, working well with hands. Turn onto lightly floured board. Gently work a few seconds until dough is formed. Pinch off pieces of dough the size of a big hazelnut and shape into small tart forms using your thumbs.

- Bake at 450° for 5 minutes. Reduce heat to 400° and bake an additional 8 to 10 minutes. Watch closely.

Yield: 35 to 40 shells

Frances Richardson

ANGEL BAVARIAN CAKE

This is a very good, light, and pretty dessert.

4 eggs, reserve whites	½ cup cold water
2 cups milk	1 teaspoon almond extract
1 tablespoon flour	1 large angel food cake, loaf
1 cup sugar	½ pint heavy cream
pinch of salt	1 coconut (optional)
1 envelope gelatin	toasted almonds (optional)

- Combine egg yolks and next four ingredients in top of a double boiler over simmering water. Do not let bottom touch water. Stir constantly until custard thickens.

- Dissolve gelatin in water; add dissolved gelatin and almond extract to hot custard. Beat egg whites until stiff and fold in.

- Cut cake into 4 long slices; line a 13x9x2-inch glass dish with 2 slices; cover with ½ of custard. Place remaining 2 slices over custard and pour remaining custard over cake slices.

- Refrigerate at least 4 hours or overnight. Whip cream, add a little sugar, if desired; spread on top and garnish with coconut and almonds.

Yield: 15 to 18 servings

Tag Wylie

POT DE CRÈME ⊂×

1 egg	1 (6-ounce) package chocolate
2 tablespoons sugar	chips
2 tablespoons rum, sherry,	¾ cup milk, scalded
brandy, or Crème de Menthe	

- Put everything in blender and blend 2 minutes.

- Pour into 6 Pot de Crème cups, demitasse cups, or short stemmed cocktail glasses. Chill overnight and serve with a dollop of whipped cream.

Yield: 6 servings

Maria Temple

TIRAMISU

Translates "Pick-me-up" in Italian.

1 (16-ounce) container of Mascarpone cheese	3 squares semi-sweet chocolate, coarsely grated, divided
½ cup powdered sugar plus 2 tablespoons, divided	½ teaspoon salt
3 tablespoons coffee liqueur plus ⅓ cup, divided	1½ cups heavy cream, divided 2 teaspoons instant espresso powder
1½ teaspoons vanilla, divided	2 tablespoon water 2 packages Italian ladyfingers

- Beat Mascarpone, ½ cup sugar, 3 tablespoons liqueur, 1 teaspoon vanilla, ⅔ cup grated chocolate, and salt in a large bowl. In a small bowl, whip 1 cup cream until soft peaks form. Fold into cheese mixture.

- Mix espresso powder, ⅓ cup liqueur, ½ teaspoon vanilla, and 2 table-spoons water. Line a 10-cup bowl with ¼ of lady fingers. Brush with 2 tablespoons of expresso mixture. Spoon ⅓ of cheese mixture on top. Repeat for 2 more layers.

- Top with ladyfingers gently pressed into cheese mixture. Brush with remaining espresso mixture. Sprinkle with remaining chocolate.

- Beat remaining ½ cup cream with 2 tablespoons powdered sugar. Spread on top. Cover with foil and chill for 4 hours or overnight.

Yield: 12 to 16 servings

This is an Italian dessert which has become very popular. You may decorate with pastry tube or sprinkle with grated chocolate or finely chopped nuts. Bonomo's Italian Groceria, 334 East Bay Street, Charleston, SC, for Mascarpone, Italian ladyfingers, and espresso powder. For Mascarpone cheese, substitute 1 cup ricotta cheese combined with ⅓ cup heavy cream in a food processor until smooth and thickened.

Sarah Eggleston

EGGNOG CAKE

Very elegant dessert. This has been served in my family for over 100 years.

1 cup butter	1 cup black walnuts, chopped
1 box powdered sugar	1 pound plain ladyfingers, split
6 eggs, separated	1 pint of heavy cream, whipped
6 tablespoons whiskey	

- Cream butter and sugar and set aside. Pour whiskey into egg yolks and beat until light in color. Add to butter and sugar mixture and mix well. Stir in nuts.

- Beat egg whites until stiff. Fold into above mixture.

- Rub bottom and sides of a large glass bowl with butter. Line bottom and sides with ladyfingers. Spread half of the mixture over ladyfingers. Repeat ladyfinger and mixture layers ending with a layer of ladyfingers.

- Chill well. Remove dessert from dish by placing bowl in a sink of warm water for a few seconds. Invert onto a dessert plate and ice with whipped cream.

Yield: 12-14 servings

Van Leer Rowe

OLD FASHIONED BOILED CUSTARD

4 eggs yolks	¼ teaspoon salt
¾ cup sugar	3 cups milk, scalded
1½ tablespoon flour	1 tablespoon vanilla

- Combine egg yolks, sugar, flour, and salt in top of a double boiler. Stir briskly. Add scalded milk and cook over boiling water, stirring constantly until custard thickens slightly.

- Remove from heat at once to avoid curdling. Strain and cool slightly. Stir vanilla into custard. Chill covered.

Yield: 1 quart

May also be used as sauce for cake or fresh fruit.

Aimee Kornegay

CHARLOTTE RUSSE

The perfect ending for a special dinner.

2 dozen ladyfingers	¼ cup cold milk
1 pint heavy cream	2 packages unflavored gelatin
5 eggs, separated	½ cup hot milk
⅔ cup sugar	1 tablespoon vanilla or
pinch of salt	4 ounces bourbon or sherry

- Split ladyfingers and line sides and bottom of 2 bowls.

- Beat cream until stiff. Set aside.

- Separate eggs. Beat yolks well and whites until stiff. Add sugar and salt to egg yolks.

- Dissolve gelatin in cold milk. Heat additional milk and add to gelatin, dissolving thoroughly. Allow this mixture to cool. Pour into yolk mixture and, while still beating, add flavoring slowly. Fold in cream, then egg whites.

- Spoon this mixture over ladyfingers. Place split ladyfingers across top. Chill overnight.

Yield: 10 to 12 servings

Aimee Kornegay

GRAND MARNIER SAUCE

Wonderful served over fresh strawberries, blueberries, or peaches.

3 egg yolks	¼ cup Grand Marnier Liqueur,
½ cup sugar	divided
	1 cup heavy cream

- Beat egg yolks and sugar in top of a double boiler until thick and pale yellow. Remove from heat and stir in half of liqueur. Refrigerate until completely cool.

- Beat cream until stiff peaks form. Fold into the cooled egg mixture; add remaining liqueur and refrigerate.

Yield: 8 servings

Van Leer Rowe

DAVID'S CHOCOLATE PECAN MOUSSE WITH SABAYON SAUCE

1 pound semi-sweet baking chocolate	½ pound puréed "Edisto" pecans
2 cups unsalted butter	1 teaspoon vanilla
5 eggs, separated and beaten	1 pint heavy cream
2 ounces Dark Bermuda Rum	4 envelopes unflavored gelatin

- Melt chocolate and butter in top of a double boiler. Set aside.

- Beat egg yolks until pale yellow. Add yolks, rum, and pecans to first mixture and mix well.

- Beat egg whites until thickened. Add chocolate mixture to whites very slowly. Add vanilla, cream, and gelatin. Mix well.

- Spoon mixture into a glass bowl. Refrigerate for 10 hours. Serve with Sabayon Sauce.

SABAYON SAUCE

5 egg yolks	¾ cup sugar
grated zest of ½ lemon	6 tablespoons Marsala
vanilla, a few drops	

- Place egg yolks, lemon zest, vanilla, and sugar in a metal bowl. Whisk until the mixture is thick and pale in color.

- Bring the water in a double boiler to a slow simmer. Place metal bowl over water in the bottom of the double boiler and continue whisking, adding Marsala, a little at a time, until the sauce is thick and frothy.

Yield: 8 servings

Francois Frederic Fisera is a professional chef from France and now lives in Columbia, South Carolina, where he owns and operates "Fleur de Lys" Home Culinary Institute. He is a frequent visitor on Edisto.

Francois Frederic Fisera

"OLE TIMEY" GINGERBREAD
WITH LEMON SAUCE

1 cup butter	4 cups flour
2 cups brown sugar	1 tablespoon ground ginger
3 eggs	1 teaspoon cinnamon
½ cup molasses	1 teaspoon baking soda
½ cup honey	1 cup milk

• Cream butter and sugar with an electric mixer until light. Add eggs, one at a time, beating well after each addition. Lower speed and add molasses and honey.

• Sift in flour, ginger, and cinnamon and blend well. Stir soda into milk and add to batter, mixing well. Turn batter into a greased 13x9x2-inch baking pan.

• Bake at 350° for 45 minutes or until cake leaves sides of pan.

• Prepare Lemon Sauce. Pour over hot gingerbread.

LEMON SAUCE

1 tablespoon cornstarch	¾ cup boiling water
¾ cup sugar	1 tablespoon butter
⅛ teaspoon salt	3 tablespoons lemon juice

• Combine cornstarch, sugar, salt, and boiling water. Bring back to a boil and cook slowly until thick. Add butter and lemon juice and cook 2 minutes longer.

Yield: 12 servings

Aimee Kornegay

BAKED FLAN WITH CARAMEL

Very easy to prepare and delicious! Your guests will be impressed.

¾ cup sugar
1 (14-ounce) can low fat
  sweetened condensed milk
⅔ cup milk

2 eggs
2 egg yolks
1 ¼ teaspoons vanilla

- Place ¾ cup sugar in a heavy saucepan and cook over medium heat, stirring constantly, until sugar melts and turns a light golden brown. Remove from heat. Pour hot mixture into six 8-ounce custard cups and let cool.

- Combine condensed milk and next 4 ingredients in container of a food processor; process 4 to 5 seconds until well blended. Pour evenly into custard cups.

- Place custard cups in a 13x9x2-inch pan; pour hot water to a depth of 1 inch into pan and cover with foil.

- Bake at 350° for 30 minutes or until a knife inserted near center comes out clean. Remove cups from water; let cool. Chill over night.

- To serve, run knife around edge of custard; invert onto dessert plates. Drizzle caramel over top. Arrange assorted fresh fruit around sides.

Yield: 6 servings

You may prepare dessert 2 to 3 days ahead.

Van Leer Rowe

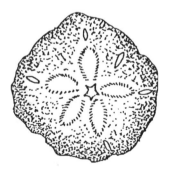

PERFECT PEACH ICE CREAM

Summer really doesn't come until we serve this wonderful treat.

4 pounds ripe peaches, pared and
    thinly sliced or mashed
½ to ¾ cup sugar
⅛ teaspoon salt
2 cups heavy cream

2 cups evaporated milk
½ cup sugar
1 teaspoon vanilla
1 package instant vanilla pudding
    mix and milk (optional)

- Combine peaches, sugar, and salt. Cover and allow to stand in refrigerator until sugar is dissolved.

- Combine cream, evaporated milk, sugar, and vanilla. Add pudding mix and milk to fill line, if desired.

- Partly churn/freeze. Add fruit mixture when half frozen and finish freezing.

Yield: 8 servings

Linda Dennis

PRALINE GRAHAMS

*With only four ingredients, these cookies are simple
and quick to make, and they taste great, too!*

1 package graham crackers
    (⅓ of a 16-ounce box)
¾ cup butter

½ cup sugar
1 cup chopped pecans

- Separate each cracker into 4 sections. Arrange in a 15x10x1-inch pan.

- Melt butter in a sauce pan. Stir in sugar and pecans. Bring to a boil. Cook 3 minutes, stirring frequently. Spread mixture evenly over crackers.

- Bake at 300° for 12 minutes. Remove from pan with spatula. Let cool on waxed paper.

Yield: 3½ dozen

Bert Hatch

EDISTO PECAN DREAM BARS

1 package yellow cake mix   ½ cup butter, melted
    less ⅔ cup   1 egg

- Reserve ⅔ cup cake mix for filling. Combine remaining cake mix, butter, and eggs; mix until crumbly. Press into a greased 13x9x 2-inch baking pan.

- Bake at 350° for 15 to 20 minutes until light golden brown.

- Prepare filling. Pour filling over partially baked crust. Return to oven. Bake 30 to 35 minutes until filling is set. Cool, cut into bars.

FILLING

⅔ cup cake mix
½ cup brown sugar, firmly packed   3 eggs
1½ cups dark corn syrup   1 cup chopped pecans
1 teaspoon rum extract

- Combine cake mix and remaining ingredients; mix well.

  Yield: 64 (1x1½-inch) bars

  These freeze up to 3 months.

  Jan Dossett
  Tommy Nease

MALE CAKES

½ cup butter, melted   1 teaspoon vanilla
2 cups light brown sugar   1 cup nuts, chopped
2 eggs   powdered sugar (optional)
½ cup flour

- Pour melted butter over sugar and stir. Add eggs, flour, vanilla, and nuts. Mix well. Pour into a greased 8x8-inch tin.

- Bake at 300° for 40 minutes until batter is firm. Cool, cut into small squares, and dust with powdered sugar.

  Yield: 2 dozen

  Gale Belser

GOOEY BARS

1 box vanilla cake mix	1 egg
½ cup margarine	

- Combine cake mix margarine and egg. Mix well and spread into a greased metal 13x9x2-inch pan.

- Prepare topping. Pour on top of batter.

- Bake at 350° for 35 to 40 minutes or until light brown. Cool and sprinkle with powdered sugar. Serve the next day.

TOPPING

1 (8-ounce) package cream cheese, softened	2 eggs
1 box powdered sugar	2 teaspoons vanilla

- Combine cream cheese, sugar, eggs, and vanilla. Beat on high speed with an electric mixer for 5 minutes.

  Yield: 36 bars

Josita Montgomery

OATMEAL COOKIES

1 cup margarine	½ teaspoon salt
1 cup sugar	1 teaspoon vanilla
1 cup brown sugar	2 cups flour
2 eggs	2 cups oatmeal (regular or quick)
1 teaspoon soda	1 cup raisins
¼ teaspoon baking powder	

- Combine margarine with remaining ingredients and mix well.

- Drop by teaspoons on greased baking sheet.

- Bake at 400° for 10 to 12 minutes. Cool on racks.

  Yield: 6 dozen

Lisa Barclay

May substitute shredded coconut or chocolate chips for raisins.

BROWNIES SAVANNAH STYLE

Everyone will love these.

½ cup margarine
1 cup sugar
4 eggs
1 teaspoon vanilla

dash of salt
1 (16-ounce) can chocolate syrup
1 cup flour

- Cream margarine and sugar until smooth. Add eggs, one at a time, beating well after each addition. Stir in vanilla and salt. Alternately add chocolate syrup and flour to creamed mixture. Beat until smooth. Pour into a greased and floured 13x9x2-inch baking pan.

- Bake at 350° for 25 to 30 minutes.

- Prepare chocolate icing. Ice brownies while hot.

CHOCOLATE ICING

6 tablespoons butter
6 tablespoons milk

¾ cup chocolate chips
2 cups powdered sugar, sifted

- Combine butter and milk in a sauce pan. Bring to a boil and boil for 2 minutes. Add the chocolate chips. Stir until melted.

- Remove from heat. Add powdered sugar and blend well.

Yield: 24 servings

Laura Wimbish

EASY OATMEAL COOKIES

1 cup butter or margarine
1 cup sugar
1 cup flour

1 teaspoon soda
2 cups quick oatmeal

- Mix butter and remaining ingredients. Roll dough into small balls and flatten on an ungreased baking sheet.

- Bake at 350° for 15 minutes or until golden brown.

Yield: 4 dozen

Selina Lyman

SNICKERDOODLES

1½ cups sugar	2 teaspoons cream of tartar
1 cup butter	1 teaspoon baking soda
2 eggs	¼ teaspoon salt
2¾ cups flour	

- Cream sugar, butter, and eggs together until smooth.

- Sift flour, cream of tartar, soda, and salt together. Add to creamed mixture. Batter will be stiff. Shape into 1-inch balls.

- Prepare sugar-cinnamon mix. Roll balls in mixture. Place on ungreased baking sheet.

- Bake at 400° for 8 to 10 minutes.

SUGAR-CINNAMON MIX

½ cup sugar	2 tablespoons cinnamon

- Mix sugar and cinnamon together.

Yield: 6 dozen (2½-inch) cookies

Cindy Kapp

TOFFEE BARS

Wey Camp's (Trinity's Rector) favorite cookie as a teenager.
Helen Coker is Wey's mother.

1 cup butter	2 cups flour
1 cup brown sugar	pinch of salt
1 teaspoon vanilla	1 cup chocolate chips
1 teaspoon maple extract	1 cup chopped pecans or walnuts

- Cream butter, sugar, and flavorings in a large bowl. Add flour and salt and mix well. Stir in chocolate chips and nuts. Spread into a 15x10x1-inch pan.

- Bake at 325° for 25 minutes until lightly browned. Cut into bars and cool in pan.

Yield: 3 to 4 dozen, depending on size of bars.

Helen Coker

DOUBLE GINGERSNAPS

A half dozen or so of these and a glass of milk and a good book on a rainy night...Life does not get any better than this!

1 cup butter
2 cups sugar
2 eggs
½ cup molasses
4 cups flour

2 teaspoons baking soda
2 teaspoons cinnamon
2 teaspoons ground cloves
4 teaspoons ground ginger
sugar for rolling

• Cream butter and sugar. Add eggs and molasses and blend well.

• Sift together flour and next 4 ingredients. Add one half of dry ingredients to creamed mixture and blend with mixer. Add remaining half of dry ingredients and blend by hand. Chill for several hours. Make walnut size balls of dough and roll in sugar. Place on ungreased baking sheet.

• Bake at 350° for 15 minutes.

Yield:5 to 6 dozen

You may bake as many cookies as you wish at one time and refrigerate or freeze the remaining dough.

Bert Hatch

TOFFEE SQUARES

These are easy to make with your children and are delicious.

1 cup butter, softened
1 cup light brown sugar
1 egg yolk

1 cup flour
6 chocolate candy bars
⅔ cup finely chopped pecans

• Cream butter and sugar until smooth. Add egg yolk and flour. Mix until well blended. Spread dough in a lightly greased 15x10x1-inch pan.

• Bake at 350° for 15 to 20 minutes or until medium brown.

• Remove from oven and put chocolate bars on top and let melt. Spread chocolate over crust carefully. Sprinkle nuts on top. Cool and cut into squares.

Yield: 3 or 4 dozen

Van Leer Rowe

STRAWBERRY COOKIES

1½ cups butter	3 cups cake flour
1 cup sugar	strawberry preserves
2 egg yolks	

- Cream butter and sugar. Add egg yolks and flour and mix well. Refrigerate.

- Shape dough into balls about the size of a marble. Press the center of each and put in a dab of strawberry preserves.

- Bake at 350° for 20 to 25 minutes. Take from oven and immediately put on brown paper (grocery bags) until cool.

Yield: 5 dozen

Keep refrigerating dough as you work with each batch of cookies. These may be made several days ahead and stored in tins.

Betty Belser

May add 1 teaspoon vanilla and substitute raspberry jam.

Belle Palmer

CARAMEL SQUARES

½ cup butter or margarine	1 teaspoon vanilla
1 package brown sugar, light or dark	¾ cup chopped nuts
3 eggs, beaten	1 cup powdered sugar
1½ cups self-rising flour	

- Melt butter and sugar together and cool slightly. Add eggs, flour, vanilla, and nuts. Mix well. Spread in a 13x9x2-inch pan.

- Bake at 325° for 40 minutes. Cool in pan. Cut in small squares and sprinkle with powdered sugar.

Yield: 36 to 48 squares

Veda Godwin

RASPBERRY SQUARES

Lou was a true and faithful member of ECW.
She brought these to all our teas and receptions.

1 package butter cake mix
½ cup nuts, chopped fine
¼ cup margarine, softened

1 egg
1 (10 or 12 ounce) jar raspberry
   preserves or jam

- Mix cake mix, nuts, margarine, and egg with electric mixer on low speed until crumbly. Press into a 13x9x2-inch greased and floured pan. Spread with preserves or jam.

- Bake at 350° for 20 to 25 minutes.

- Prepare glaze. Let cake cool and drizzle with glaze. Let glaze set, cut into squares.

GLAZE

½ cup powdered sugar
2½ teaspoons water

½ teaspoon almond extract

- Mix sugar, water, and almond extract in small bowl.

Yield: 48 squares

These are good kept cold in refrigerator.

Lou Whitmore

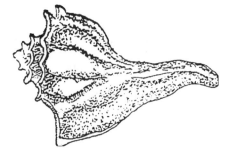

CRYSTALLIZED VIOLETS

One bunch freshly picked violets
Two drops almond extract
One egg white
One tablespoonful water
One half cup powdered sugar

Wash violets thoroughly — drain on absorbent paper — combine egg white and water — beat slightly — add extract — brush on petals with pastry brush — be sure to cover all parts — sprinkle with powdered sugar — covering completely — place on cake rack covered with wax paper — dry in 200 degree oven 20 to 30 minutes — store in glass jars.

Gaillard Original

MOCK HEATH BARS

1 cup butter	1 (12-ounce) package chocolate
1 cup brown sugar, packed	chips
35 saltine crackers	

- Bring butter and sugar to a boil and boil 5 minutes.

- Line a 15x10x1-inch pan with foil and 35 crackers; pour butter mixture on crackers.

- Bake at 350° for 5 minutes.

- Sprinkle with chips; spread when melted.

- Refrigerate and when hard, break into pieces.

  Yield: 70 pieces

  May sprinkle with 1 cup finely chopped pecans.

  Veda Godwin, Cathy Richardson

NEVER FAIL FUDGE

¼ cup margarine	18 large marshmallows
1 (12-ounce) can evaporated milk	1 teaspoon vanilla
4 cups sugar	1 cup chopped pecans
2 (12-ounce) packages	
chocolate chips	

- Combine margarine, milk, and sugar in a saucepan and bring to a boil. Stir until a firm ball forms when dropped in a cup of water.

- Remove from heat and add chips, marshmallows, and vanilla. Beat until stiff. Add nuts and pour into a greased 13x9x2-inch pan.

- Chill for 2 hours and cut into squares.

  Yield: 72 squares

  Veda Godwin

PRALINES

3 cups sugar, divided   2 cups pecan halves
1 cup milk

- Combine 2 cups sugar with milk in a large heavy saucepan.

- Brown the remaining cup of sugar in a non-stick saucepan until caramel colored.

- Bring milk mixture to a slow boil. Add caramelized sugar. Cook to a soft ball stage (238°) and add nuts.

- Remove from heat and beat, beat, beat until thickened.

- Drop by spoonfuls onto wax paper and let harden.

  Yield: 2 dozen

Caroline Watson

ENGLISH TOFFEE

Excellent!

2 cups butter   12 ounces chocolate chips
2 cups sugar   1 cup finely chopped pecans
2 tablespoons water

- Combine butter, sugar, and water in a large heavy bottom saucepan. Heat stirring constantly until mixture is a deep caramel color.

- Pour into a greased 15x10x1-inch jelly-roll pan. Sprinkle with chips and spread when melted. Sprinkle with nuts.

- Cool completely; break into pieces.

  Yield: 70 pieces

Aimee Nelson

"THE" TREE

Bon appétit from 'Pon Top Edisto!

'PON TOP EDISTO

CONTRIBUTORS

"Thanks be to God!" for the members and friends of Trinity who so generously contributed their favorite recipes, talents, and time to 'PON TOP EDISTO. Due to the lack of space, we were unable to use all of your recipes. We apologize.

The Cookbook Committee

Jacquelyn C. (Jackie) Adams
Johanne Albright
Sarah Richardson Arnold
Catherine Arnot
George W. Arnot
Tina Atwood
LePage (Pagie) Bailey
Adelaide Bailey
Kathryn Bailey
Lisa Barclay
Philip Bardin
Beth M. Barker
David Barker
Louise Barwick
Steve Beattie
Mary Alice Beck
Betty Belser
Gale Belser
Ritchie Belser
Anne Berlin
Randolph W. Berretta
Les Blankin
Rosa Townsend Blankin
Rosie Hutson Blankin
Caroline C. Boineau
C. C. (Jack) Boineau
Sarah Bolton
Ramona J. Bosserman
Mary Elizabeth Boykin
Debbie Brockman
Jorga Broome
Pink Brown
Lucille Bryant
Anthony (Tony) Burke
Earnestine Burnell
Mary Margaret Calk

E. Weyman (Ed) Camp, III
E. Weyman (Wey) Camp, IV
Melissa T. (Missy) Camp
Karen L. Carter
Helen M. Clarkson
N. Heyward Clarkson, III
Helen O. Coker
Virginia Pope (Ginny) Cole
Amy Connor
Parker E. Connor, Jr.
Ann Cowsert
Alex S. Crawford
Mary Crawford
Annabelle Creech
Sally Currin
Robert G. (Bob) Currin, Jr.
Jane Curtan
Linda Dennis
R. Wightman (Bob) Dibble, Jr.
Ruth D. Dodge
Marie T. (Timmy) Dorn
Janeth N. (Jan) Dossett
Denise Driggers
Kenneth (Kenny) Driggers
Debbie DuBose
Bruce B. Earnshaw
Tecla Earnshaw
Sarah Mikell Eggleston
Mary Sue Ellis
Mary Elliott Fersner
Weesie Fickling
Francois Fisera
Bouchie Fontaine
Sallie J. Fontaine
Evelyn Ford
Carol K. Fowles

CONTRIBUTORS (continued)

James H. Fowles, Jr.
David L. Foxworth
Joan Foxworth
Samuel Ravenel (Sammy) Gaillard
David Gallup
Virginia Mixson Geraty
E. David Gibbons
Cornelia D. (Nela) Gibbons
Terry Girdauskas
Veda Godwin
Doris Gramling
Dorothy (Dot) Gressette
Tatum Gressette, Jr.
George Gross
Pauline Gross
Virginia D. (Ginny) Guerard
Frances R. Guy
Mary Ella Hackett
William E. (Bill) Hackett
Joan Halliday
Barbara W. Hamlen
Barbara K. Harmon
Bert H. Hatch
Evelyn S. (Ebby) Hatch
Mercia Hayes
Mary Ann Heath
Phyllis Herrick
Laura Hewitt
William B. (Bill) Hewitt
Sue Highfield
William (Billy) Hiott
Jean Rowe Hiott
Barbara G. Hood
William C. (Bill) Hood
William C. (Chip) Hood, Jr.
Jackie B. Houser
Morgan Houser
John B. (Demi) Howard
Eleanor V. (Ellie) Howard
Kerry Howard
Pegge Howard
Madeline Hackett Huffines
Gwendolyn (Gwen) Hughes
Katherine Otis (Kat) Hunt
Alice L. Hutson

Harry C. Hutson
Kitty Jenkins Hutson
Ann Hutto
Fred Inman
Judy Inman
Naomi Irwin
E. Darrell Jervey
Patricia H. (Pat) Jervey
Cynthia B. (Cindy) Kapp
Thomas L. (Tom) Kapp
Dorothy Keach
Lorraine Kirchner
Marie Bost Kizer
Aimee Reese Kornegay
John D. Kornegay
John D. Kornegay, Jr.
Mary Pat Kornegay
Lucile M. (Bo) Lachicotte
Chip Lachicotte
Jenifer Lachicotte
Leslie Blankin Lang
Robert E. (Bobo) Lee
Frances McD. Leitner
Cindy Lenz
Brenda Lewis
N.C. (Nick) Lindsay
Selina K. Lyman
Edith (Muff) Lyons
William E. Lyons
Burnet R. Maybank, Jr.
Burnet R. Maybank, III
Marian M. Maybank
Jane M. McCollum
Reba McGowan
Virginia McWhirter
Henrietta McWillie
Agnes Messemer
Elizabeth E. (Eliza) Messersmith
John Messersmith
Alicia H. Mikell
I. Jenkins (Jenks) Mikell, Jr.
Mary Eleanor Mitchell
Felix Montgomery
Josita M. Montgomery
Rose Jenkins Montgomery
Aimee Kornegay Moore
Elizabeth F. Moore

CONTRIBUTORS (continued)

Delores (Dee) Moss
Larry H. Moss
Maria K. Mungo
Steven W. Mungo
Marian C. Murray
Ora Dell Murray
Barbara Myers
Ann Nease
Thomas E. (Tom) Nease
Aimee Kornegay (Petey) Nelson
Brian A. Nelson
John R. Nye
Judith Reese (Judie) Nye
Frances Oxner
Belle C. Palmer
Ann Parler
Margaret M. (Peggy) Pepper
Harmon B. Person
Joyce L. Person
Anne C. Peterson
Thomas J. (Tom) Peterson
Walter Prause
Clair Price
Jan Rasmussen
Aimee Urguhart Reese
Jesse T. Reese, Jr.
Jesse T. Reese, III
Leigh S. Reese
Jean Reid
Elva W. Richards
Cantey Richardson
Cathy Richardson
Frances M. (Cotton) Richardson
Francis McG. Richardson
Meredith Richardson
Rob Richardson
Janet Roberts
Mildred Ann Rodwell
Andrew H. (Andy) Rowe
Gina Rowe
Van Leer C. Rowe
Walker E. (Buddy) Rowe, Jr.
Walton D. Salley
Susalee N. Sasser
William C. (Bill) Sasser

Katherine Settle
Bronnie Smith
Laura Smith
Elizabeth (Beth) A. Smoak
Annie F. (Nan) Steadman
Morris E. (Bud) Steadman
Joe Steadman
Margaret B. (Peg) Stover
Marion Sullivan
Evangeline P. (Vangie) Summers
Maria Temple
Elinor Thompson
John A. Thompson, Jr.
V. V. Kornegay Thompson
Katherine Tillinghast
Judy Tomlin
Amy U. Trowell
Wallace W. Trowell
Trinity ECW
Courtney Tutas
W. Parker Tuten, Jr.
Suzanne M. Tuten
Gene Ulmer
Ellen Unger
H. Wayne (Bubba) Unger, Jr.
Doris Upshur
Carolina L. Watson
Polly Welsh
Faith Wendling
Katherine (Kitsy) Westmoreland
Amelia (Mimi) Whaley
Rebecca Whaley
Roger B. Whaley, Jr.
Martha B. Whetstone
Lou Whitmore
Laura Wimbish
Shannon Winton
Grace Woodhead
Gertrude Bailey Woods
Curtis W. Worthington
Floride McD. Worthington
E. S. (Tag) Wylie
Elizabeth H. Young
Joseph (Joe) Young
Helen Youngblood
Jan Zehr

'PON TOP EDISTO
ARTISTS

SAMUEL RAVENEL GAILLARD
516 Central Avenue
Summerville, SC 29483

SOUTH CAROLINA LOWCOUNTRY PRINTS AVAILABLE

V. GUERARD
Virginia Guerard
2702 Point Street
Edisto Beach, SC 29438

COVER PRINT AVAILABLE
Full print includes side yard of church.

ELIZABETH ALLSTON SMOAK
Represented by
WITH THESE HANDS
1444 Highway 174
Edisto Island, SC 29438
and
ST. PAUL'S COMMUNITY MARKETING CENTER
Adams Run, SC 29426
Gullah Books & Tapes
Prints & Original Paintings

AMELIA WHALEY WATERCOLORS
31 New Street
Charleston, SC 29401
Represented by
COURTYARD ART GALLERY
195½ King Street
Charleston, SC 29401

All art is copyrighted by the respective artists.

270

Index

271

Index

'Pon Top Edisto

Index

Index

Index

Index

'Pon Top Edisto

Index

'Pon Top Edisto

'PON TOP EDISTO
Trinity Episcopal Church
P.O. Box 425
Edisto Island, SC 29438

Please send _____ copies   @ $17.95 each _____

Shipping and Handling   @ $5.00 each _____

                                                Total _____

Name _____

Address _____

City _____ State _____ Zip _____

Please make check payable to:

'PON TOP EDISTO

'PON TOP EDISTO
Trinity Episcopal Church
P.O. Box 425
Edisto Island, SC 29438

Please send _____ copies   @ $17.95 each _____

Shipping and Handling   @ $5.00 each _____

                                                Total _____

Name _____

Address _____

City _____ State _____ Zip _____

Please make check payable to:

'PON TOP EDISTO

NOTES